"WAITER, THERE'S A FLY IN MY SOUP"

● ● ● ● ● ● ● ● ●

"Waiter, There's a Fly in My Soup"

• • • • • • • • • • • • • •

HOW TO MAKE
MEGABUCKS
WAITING TABLES

• • • • • • • • • • • • • •

LESLIE N. LEWIS

BOOKMARK PUBLISHING CORP.
NEW YORK, 1997

Published by **BOOKMARK PUBLISHING CORP.**
PO Box 2100, Amagansett, NY 11930

Produced for **BOOKMARK PUBLISHING CORP.** by
TENTH AVENUE EDITIONS, INC.
625 Broadway, Suite 903
New York, NY 10012
Creative Director: Clive Giboire
Managing Editor: Suzanne Cobban
Associate Editor: Judy Gelman Myers

Cover Design by: Tenth Avenue Editions, Inc.
Cover Illustration: Keith Knight

ISBN: 1-880808-05-6

0 9 8 7 6 5 4 3 2

Manufactured in the United States of America

For the memory of
my Father and Great-grandfather

CONTENTS

PART I: INTRODUCTION

PART II: GETTING HIRED

PART III: TRICKS OF THE TRADE

PART IV: SOME POTENTIAL PROBLEMS

PART V: CONCLUSION

EXTRAS

**Thanks to everyone
who helped me with this book!
Especially:**

Jessica Ambats, Dawn Bargamian, Ly Bolia, Daryl Brown, Marie D. Brown, Angela Cappetta, Suzanne Cobban, Bursten Marsteller, Michael Cohn, Amerita Ford, Clive Giboire, Millie Gilliard, the staff at Grendel's Den in Cambridge, Vanessa Grigoriadis, the staff at the House of Blues in Cambridge, Steven Hunt, Leslie Jowett, Stephanie King, Keith Knight, Dahlia Loeb, Genevieve Lohman, Butch Meily, Lauren Monaco, Judy Gelman Myers, Rosalie O'Brien, DoLen Perkins, Alain Pesce, Tony Puche and the staff at News Café in Miami Beach, I-fan Quirk, Peter Rooney, Joe Sabah, Jim and Linda Salisbury, Tom Shelford, Michael Stillman, the staff at Tenth Avenue Editions in New York, Gavin Sword, Marc Zelanco, Joseph Fugett, Christina S. N. Lewis, and Loida N. Lewis, whose idea it was in the first place.

PART I

INTRODUCTION

DO YOU WANT TO MAKE GOOD MONEY in a job that requires little more from you than some common sense? Hang out with fun young people who like to party both at work and after? Have experiences that will make great material for your memoirs? Then waiting tables is for you.

When I started as a waitress at the fun and funky News Café in Miami Beach, I didn't know the first thing about the job, and boy, did it show. The employee manual was helpful, but there was so much more to learn in order to do the job well, make money, and keep my sanity, too. I started asking experienced waiters for all the tips they could tell me so I would have a clue about how to handle the job. Something must have worked, because in my second month at the restaurant, I was offered a management position! I had received so much helpful advice from coworkers that I decided to do more extensive research and turn what I had learned into a book.

"Waiter, There's a Fly in My Soup" is written for young people who need a job that doesn't ask too much of them. If you can master this job, you'll have the opportunity to make lots of money with minimal mental work. You'll also meet tons of new friends (and some pretty quirky people as well). My aim is to show you how to get hired and what to do once you get your foot in the door. You'll be a MegaBucks-making, manager pleasing, schmooze-meister in no time at all.

WHY YOU MIGHT WANT TO WAIT TABLES

1
GOOD MONEY

This is the biggest lure the service industry has to offer. The money is amazing. Really, I'm not lying. If you get a job at a decent restaurant, you can make upwards of \$100/shift. Some people have supported themselves through graduate school by waiting tables—not bad for a job that in itself requires no degrees at all! Which, of course, brings us to the next point.

2
NO DEGREES REQUIRED

In fact, you don't even necessarily need any experience (especially, ahem, since you now have this book to tell you what you need to know). Anyone can wait tables, even if you're a sophomore in high school or have never been gainfully employed before.

3
FLEXIBILITY I:
CAN BE DONE ANYTIME, ANYWHERE

You can wait tables anywhere. You could even leave the country and wait tables—the requirements don't change much from restaurant to restaurant. All you need is the basic knowledge.

Other bonuses about your new job waiting tables: You can quit at the drop of a hat with no major repercussions. And if your manager is cool, you could even take off for the Ivory Coast for three months and return to your old job!

Finally, the hours are flexible. You can go to auditions during the day and wait tables at night. Or, you can make waiting tables into your proverbial "day job", and keep your evenings free to sing in nightclubs or what-have-you.

4
FLEXIBILITY II:
COVERING AND PICKING UP SHIFTS

As I've pointed out, you can basically be an idiot and be a successful waiter. Therefore, any random you work with can switch shifts with you. You can give away your Saturdays or pick up your coworker's Tuesdays. For example, you get a hot date for the night—you don't want to say no (it might illustrate lack of interest)—so, you try to get your shift covered. Chances are, it'll be a cinch. Hang a sign, call a coworker, or if all else fails, go in to work at the shift change-over and beg! Your coworkers will dig the opportunity to make some extra money, and all you have to do is return the favor sometime. This job is unparalleled in its flexibility.

5
IT'S KINDA FUN!

Most of the time (unless you're waiting tables at a four-star restaurant, and you would clearly not be reading this book if that were the case) you're working with fun, young people. You can hang before work, during work, and after work—instant friends!

6
YIPPEE, A UNIFORM

With a uniform, you don't have to worry about what to wear—you wear what they tell you to! You can wear the same clothing to work over and over again. (You should definitely wash it, though.)

7
CHEAP EATS

You can save on food costs, since you usually have the opportunity to eat at the restaurant. Most restaurants give free or discounted food to their staff, and it's in your best interest to take advantage of this deal.

Also, if you get in good with the cooks, you can learn new and interesting ways to make food.

A WAITER'S FRIDGE

Until the term "waitron" is accepted as the industry standard gender-neutral term, I will refer to both male and female service staff as "waiters" even though that appelation usually refers to a server of the male persuasion. Write your congress-persun about the cause for the "waitron."

Drawbacks of Waiting Tables

EVERY JOB HAS ITS NEGATIVES, and the restaurant industry is no exception. Here are some of the downsides of waiting tables that you should keep in mind while embarking on your new employment path.

1
SERVILITY MAY NOT BE YOUR THING

You have to serve people. Some people find this demeaning, irritating, annoying, etc. If you can't deal with serving people, this may not be the job for you.

2
YOU PROBABLY DON'T HAVE A CONTRACT

You have no job security at all. You can be fired at the drop of a hat, regardless of how long you've been working at the place.

3
WACKO PATROL

You have to deal with all kinds of crazy people, and I do not limit this to the people you're waiting on. Ask anyone who has ever waited tables before: Managers, owners and other waiters can be the weirdest of the bunch.

4
UNPREDICTABLE CASH FLOW

You never know how much money you're going to make. Some days you'll walk home with enough money from that shift to pay half your rent. Other days, you're lucky if you have a dollar for the bus ride home, and you'll feel like a character in some novel titled *The Unbearable Lightness of Being Undertipped*. It's random.

It takes a certain personality type to be a successful waiter. Dealing with customer demands, crazy schedules, and random occurrences takes patience, dedication, and motivation. So, with that in mind, let's take a little personality test to see if you have what it takes to be a waiter.

THE MEGABUCKS WAITER PERSONALITY QUIZ

1. Your mother asks you to take out the garbage, your father tells you to start your homework, your sister wants you to fix her dollhouse, and your friend is waiting outside for you to go Rollerblading. You:

  a) throw a tantrum and pound your head against the wall until they take you to the hospital.

  b) take out the garbage after telling dad you'll start your homework ASAP, warning your sister that she'll have to wait for the dollhouse doctor, and shooing your friend away because you'll blade with her later.

  c) take off with your buddy 'cause that's what you wanted to do in the first place.

2. A bum passes you on the street and makes a random mean comment about your appearance. You:

  a) start to whimper.

  b) tell him to shove it, and get into a swearing match.

  c) ignore him (but glare).

3. At parties, you:

  a) entertain your friends with crazy stories you picked up from the comedy channel.

  b) gravitate toward the punch bowl and alternate between the refreshment table and the bathroom all night.

  c) have fun with a couple of pals.

4. What does your room look like?
   a) A place for everything and everything in its place.
   b) A place for everything and everything all over
      the place.
   c) A balance between calm and catastrophe.

5. You've been planning a road trip to New Orleans for weeks when, a day before the trip, your traveling partner's car breaks down and you have to find some other way to get to Mardi Gras. You:
   a) yell at your friend and wait for him to fix the problem.
   b) start polling your friends for available cars, or at
      least bus fare.
   c) decide to stay home.

6. How often do you go out to eat in a sit-down-and-let-somebody-serve-you restaurant?
   a) Daily.
   b) Weekly.
   c) Monthly.
   d) Rarely.

7. When you do go out to eat,
   a) you can tell when the server is having a bad day.
   b) you couldn't care less whether the server is having
      a bad day.

8. Are you friendly?
   a) Golly, yes!
   b) Sure.
   c) Who wants to know?

9. Your friends think you're
   a) good-looking.
   b) interesting looking.

10. How much do you smile?
    a) A lot.
    b) A little.
    c) Not much.

11. People from backgrounds different from yours
    a) make you nervous.
    b) make you laugh.
    c) make good friends.

Now, compare your answers to the key below, and count the Ws and NWs you have.

W stands for Waiter. NW stands for Not Waiter.

1. a) NW b) W c) NW	6. a) W b) W c) W d) NW
2. a) NW b) NW c) W	7. a) W b) NW
3. a) W b) NW c) W	8. a) W b) W c) NW
4. a) W b) NW c) W	9. a) W b) NW
5. a) NW b) W c) NW	10. a) W b) W c) NW
	11. a) NW b) W c) W

If you have mostly Ws, congratulations! You have many of the personality traits it takes to be a good waiter. You are patient, responsible, assertive, good-looking, organized, persuasive, entertaining, calm, and you have a strong sense of what good service in a restaurant should be.

    If you have mostly NWs, this may not be the job for you. You most likely have a quick temper, or are easily upset. Not to insult you, but you may not be very friendly or interesting. You might want to do a bit of a personality adjustment before interviewing for this job—or you can always apply for a management position!

How to
Use This Book

MY AIM IS TO SHARE my wisdom with those who have either never waited tables before or who have just started and are running into some problems. I am not the Waitress Goddess, but I'm hoping that some of my advice will help you relax and enjoy your new job. With my help, you'll be able to make the most of uncomfortable situations and have a blast while making great money.

Part II, Getting Hired, will help you gainfully gain employment at the restaurant of your choice. It will clue you into the things managers are looking for, and what to do when you go in for an interview. In **Part III, Tricks of the Trade**, I'll impart all the important tidbits you need to know to be a good waiter who can turn tables, make cash, and, of course, have fun. **Part IV, Potential Problems**, will warn you about all the obstacles you may run into on the job, including a list of things that will get you fired if you do them. The **Extras** section has helpful things like a glossary of frequently used

terms in the industry, places that are magnets for migrant waitstaff, lists of common food preparation terms, and basic wine information.

After reading this book, you'll be ready to conquer the table-waiting world.

"Waiter, There's a Fly in My Soup" can be read in a number of ways. I'll give you some suggestions: You can read it from cover to cover, savoring every word the way a starved restaurant patron savors his filet mignon. But that's really not necessary and you probably won't do it, anyway. Instead, you can read the parts you need most, like how to get hired, what to do when you get hit on by your manager, etc., as these issues pop up. Or, finally, you can skim through everything, then come back to read the tips when you've waited tables for a little bit and have identified areas you need to work on.

But most of all, have fun, and don't stress. You'll make money, I promise.✤

✤ This does not constitute a guarantee.

PART II

GETTING HIRED

BEFORE ONE CAN START MAKING THE BIG BUCKS, one must have a job. Here's how to get the one you want. This section is like your personalized copy of *What Color is Your Apron? Getting the Waitron Job You Crave.*

WHAT SEASON ARE YOU ENTERING?

OFTEN, THE EASIEST WAY TO GET A JOB waiting tables is to begin your search at the start of a big vacation season in a touristy area. If you're like most of the people who read this book, you're probably looking for a job during your summer vacation from school. So let's start with that job market.

SUMMER WORK

A resort town with a beach, mountain, or some other inspiring landmark is a mecca for tourists and the seasonal workers who will serve them. You can be one of the migrant waitstaff who converge upon these locales to bleed the vacationers dry, but only if you get there early enough to snag a coveted job.

Restaurants in summer vacation spots usually start hiring in May, and fill most of their spots by mid-June. After that, the only reason they hire additional people is if someone gets fired or quits. Finding places to work late in the season is difficult, so the earlier you get there to apply for a job, the better your chance. If you do decide to wait until later in the season to get hired, be prepared to spend a lot of time and energy getting the job you want.

WINTER WORK

Ski resorts and sunny shores are the tourist magnets in the winter, and you can make tons of money riding the cold-weather rush. Again, your chances of getting hired for seasonal winter work are better if you get there early in the season, as in pre-Thanksgiving. By New Year's Eve, most places have completed the bulk of their hiring, but again, you can always hope for somebody to get fired!

One caution: Tourist work has even less job security than regular waiter stints. A lot of people are looking for good seasonal restaurant jobs, and if you mess up, dozens are willing to fill your slot in a jiffy. Also, once the rush is over, seasonal staff is usually the first to get laid off. This may not bother you, since after the summer's done, you're headed back to school anyway. But keep in mind that if you show dedication to a seasonal job, you could come back year after year to the same job until you don't want to anymore.

To locate fantastic winter or summer tourist areas, check page 118.

Qualities to Look for in a Restaurant

(if you are lucky enough to be picky)

WHEN EXPLORING JOB OPPORTUNITIES, take the time to find out the answers to the following five issues.

1
VOLUME

Will you be making money? Will your section be filled? Or will you be picking lint out of your ears? And, though it's not in your job description, during slow shifts your manager can make you do manual labor. I've had to get up on ladders and scrub kitchen walls even though I was only getting paid the waitstaff wage of $2.75 an hour, and no one was tipping me on my creative use of Ajax. My manager told me, "You can lean? You can clean." Find a busy place, and you'll do less leaning, less cleaning.

If you do your research before going into a job search, you can find out the most popular and populated restaurants in the area where you'd like to work. You should also be able to feel the "energy" of the staff, and decide whether you would like to be a member of their team. Have a meal at a couple of those popular restaurants so you can gauge the servers' actions and attitudes, and how they all get along. Places with a steady flow of customers will be your wish list. In the same way that high school students have their "reach" colleges, as well as their safety and target schools, you can have "reach" restaurants (like the House of Blues) and even safeties (McDonald's or your uncle's diner).

2
MANAGERS

What is the management style, and does it fit with your own style? This can be a tough quality to judge, but the more you can evaluate this, the better. Is the place very petty, with annoying rules for every little action? Do the managers have real decision-making power, or are they mere puppets for the overbearing owners? Will you be worked to death by managers who schedule you for two weeks straight with no days off? How easy is it to get fired from this restaurant? Is there a good relationship between the managers and the waitstaff? FYI—there should always be a decent rapport between the staff and the managers if you don't want a hellish experience. Are the managers jerks? Needless to say, try not to work for jerks.

3
PERKS

Perks are a key aspect to any job. Of course, the most important "perk" is that you have a paying job, but the following extras can sweeten the deal. Ask: What are the side benefits working here? Is there an employee discount on food when you're not working? If you're in a ski area, does the job come with lift-tickets for the season? Does the management let you swap shifts? How long do you have to work there before you get medical coverage?

4
STATUS

Will you be proud, or, at least, not embarrassed to tell people where you work? Liking your place of employment and believing that it's a good establishment to work in will keep your spirits higher than if you're stuck slinging hash at the local drive-thru. Don't underestimate the power of name recognition: Even though you're doing the same job, you will probably feel cooler telling people you work at the hottest restaurant in town than at the Hamburger Patty. Also, be sure to check out the staff. Do they look like people that you could hang with? Because you will be seeing a lot of them, even if only on your break.

5
FAMILY PLACE?

When looking for a place to work, you may want to be wary of the family owned and managed restaurant. These smaller restaurants tend to be more micromanaged than their corporate counterparts. Understandably, when owners are managers, they can be more concerned with the nit-picky costs. They harp on things that seem inconsequential to you but mean big things to their bottom line. You'd probably be the same way if you owned the place, but you may not be psyched to deal with that from a manager. So avoid small owner-is-the-manager restaurants if you think that saving and reusing paper napkins, etc., will irritate you.

PREPARATION FOR AN INTERVIEW

MAKE SURE YOU'RE READY to get a good job by following these guidelines.

1
RÉSUMÉ

If you've ever waited tables or worked in a restaurant at all, then by all means, stick your experience on a piece of paper with an address and phone number, and hand it to your potential employer. But since you are reading this book, you probably don't have too much experience—so forget the résumé. Restaurants have applications for that anyway.

2
RECONNAISSANCE

Once you target your restaurants, find out who the key manager is. The answer is easily achieved by making a phone call to the restaurant and asking for the personnel manager's name. Don't leave your name, though. Let surprise be on your side so you can dazzle the manager by knowing her name when you meet her. Schmooze, schmooze!

3
INTERVIEW ETIQUETTE

Dress neatly. A good guideline is to look as if you're going on a date to a movie. Nothing too sleazy, though.

When you go to the interview, make sure that you bring a pen and paper. You must, must, must remember to bring a pen to the restaurant. I heard a horror story about a manager who would immediately throw out the application if the would-be waiter came unprepared. He said it illustrated a lack of seriousness about getting a job, and a lack of knowledge—a waiter always has a pen and paper, he says. And he's the one doing the hiring.

Ergo, look good and go prepared.

4
TIMING

Never apply to a restaurant during their busy hours. Managers have no time to review applications or talk to candidates in the middle of a lunch rush. Additionally, you will look clueless: Anyone who has worked in a restaurant before would know this unwritten rule! So, when targeting your restaurant, figure out a time when they are the least busy, and inquire about a job then. For most restaurants, this is early in the week (Monday to Thursday) and in the morning before lunch or in the mid-afternoon before dinner (9 A.M. to 11 A.M. and 3 P.M. to 5:30 P.M.).

5
HOW TO ACT

Be enthusiastic, be willing, and be persistent. If you have no experience, you will have more trouble convincing a manager that you are competent enough to do the job. This is why you have to emphasize your enthusiasm and your willingness to work your butt off to learn the business. Eagerness shows that you are flexible and easygoing, which managers love because it makes their job easier.

Be persistent. Restaurant managers are extremely busy people who get inundated with waitstaff applications and a ton of other concerns on a daily basis. Come back in to the restaurant, call the manager—do something to make yourself stand out from the ten other applications that the manager has in his file. One waiter went into the same restaurant every other week for over four months until the manager finally broke down and gave him a job. In the end, his persistence paid off. Sure, he felt like a dork who couldn't get a date, but he's gainfully employed, right?

WHAT MANAGERS ARE LOOKING FOR

(And How to Show Them You Have It)

I INTERVIEWED SEVERAL long-time restaurant managers and asked them what characteristics they look for in staff when they hire people. Here's what they said they want their candidates to have:

EXPERIENCE
AN EAGER ATTITUDE
A SENSE OF HONESTY
A SENSE OF RESPONSIBILITY

Here are ways of showing your interviewer that you have these things so you will get hired.

1
EXPERIENCE

On your application, you will be asked about your previous four years of work experience. Now, perhaps you picked sand out of your butt for an entire summer. No matter, you can still figure out something creative or motivated to say here.

For example, even if the only productive thing you did last summer was sell lemonade for 10¢ a glass, write creatively about this entrepreneurial adventure. (You are more than welcome to exaggerate . . . everyone does.) You don't have to mention that you operated at a loss, or that the whole production was really your five-year-old cousin's endeavor. You can make it sound like you're not a die-hard slacker, for heaven's sake.

Don't out-and-out lie about your experience by saying that you've waited tables before when you haven't, though. Even if you read this book from cover to cover and translate it into Swahili, it will still be clear that you're a newcomer when you first start on the job, and no one likes a liar. Creatively highlight your experiences, yes. Lie, no.

2
AN EAGER ATTITUDE

Managers want someone happy, helpful, willing, and able. They want a responsible person who will get the job done, and who has a good attitude to boot. So smile, be excited, and be eager. This should apply not only to interviews that you may have in the service industry but to *any* interview. Most managers want someone who will do the job well, but if that person is fun and easy to work with, so much the better.

3
HONESTY

Though honesty is hard to "prove" in an initial interview, it is important that you not seem sketchy in your first meeting with your potential employers. Be upfront and honest in all your dealings with your manager and they'll make you employee of the month.

4
RESPONSIBILITY

Be an adult, even if you're still a minor. To show you are responsible, look over all those jobs you listed under Experience on the application. There must be something that shows you lived up to your responsibilities. Think about this something before you go into your interview so you can have a handy topic to discuss. You'll look organized, motivated, and hey, you get to brag about how good you are with no one around to contradict you!

ON YOUR FIRST DAY

CONGRATULATIONS! YOU GOT HIRED! Now the fun begins. Here are some tips on what to do on your first day at work.

WEAR COMFORTABLE SHOES

Though most restaurants have a uniform, decisions about what shoes to wear are usually up to the employee. Find comfortable ones! You'll be on your feet for hours, and if your shoes aren't comfy, you'll be cursing yourself the next morning! Waiters tend to prefer sneakers, boots like Doc Martens, or anything with a cushioning sole. Fashion does not really matter for shoes in this job—comfort is the #1 priority.

GET REST BEFORE YOU GO INTO WORK

In the couple of hours before your shift starts, relax. Read a book, watch TV, or take a nap. Don't run errands all day with your final task being your first day of work. Take it easy in the few hours before your new shift begins—you will be more prepared, less stressed, and less harried for your first day. So don't try to do it all on the first day of work, like buying your uniform and opening a bank account, mailing a few packages, and then coming in to the restaurant. You'll be exhausted.

SMILE, SMILE, SMILE!

You got the job, so be happy! Even if you're messing up on your first day, keep smiling. Especially since the next chapter will help you minimize your mistakes, improve your level of service, and give you something to really smile about: Money!

PART III

TRICKS OF THE TRADE

WAITING TABLES IS BY NO MEANS rocket science, but not being aware of the "tricks of the trade" can easily send you on a miserable downward spiral. The sooner you learn to use these tricks to your benefit, the faster the money will roll in. Your table waiting life will be easier, and you won't feel crazy frazzled the way you felt your first day.

Rule #1: You are a server. Let's break that down. The waiter's most important role is to serve the customers. And, no matter how many people tell you differently, **you can gauge your performance by your tips**. If you're making great money, chances are you're a fantastic waiter—that statement inverses nicely as well.

The most important commodities that you, as a waiter, can offer to your customers are your personality, your exemplary quality of service, and your time. To be the best (or at least make the most money) you should be able to combine all three with a fun personality, great service, and an astute sense of timing. But, I won't lie to you—when you start out, your most important asset is your time and how you manage it. Okay, your personality is also important and can sometimes make up for deficient service. But in general, you should not depend too heavily on your cuteness making up for your crappy service.

Your time is very limited. Your customers' demands are never. There are only so many things you can do while waiting on six tables at the same time, and most customers don't really care if you are running around "trying your hardest." They want the best service that they can get—you are simply their pawn. The only things you have control over as a waiter is your own time and how you decide to process everyone else's demands on your time. Therefore, anticipating your customers' needs, and thereby *managing their requirements of you* is the key to becoming an efficient waiter.

Ooh, that's so important that I'm going to repeat it and put it in bigger type:

> **Anticipating your customers'
> needs, and thereby *managing
> their requirements of you* is
> the key to becoming
> an efficient waiter.**

The tips in this chapter should help you anticipate any needs your customer may have. Use these Tricks of the Trade as a basic reference, flipping through the different sections to see what you need most.

If you're new to this lovely lifestyle and have just started the job, you'll definitely want to read **The Basics** thoroughly. This will help you understand and anticipate the minimum job requirements of waiting tables. **Working with People** shows you whom to get along with, and how.

Big Tips on Makin' Big Tips has all the tricks that can help make the job a cakewalk. **Key Skills** lists the talents that most good waiters rely upon. These last two sections will be most helpful if you reread and digest them once you have a solid footing and a little familiarity of your restaurant. You can also use these sections to increase your level of service.

Client Server tells you all you need to know about treating your customers right, even when they're in the wrong. Remember the saying "The customer is always right"? Well, we abide by it, even though it may be the most annoying quote ever. **Client Server** gives you the most practical advice about dealing with the people who pay your wages—customers. Rereading during your first few weeks as a waiter will help you become a MegaBucks waiter, earning the serious dollars!

LUNCH IN THE CIA DINING ROOM

THE BASICS

WHAT ARE THE CRUCIAL ELEMENTS of the kick-butt and make-that-cash waiter? Read this section to uncover the essential attitude for the business, as well as your unofficial job description, daily itinerary, and insider information on industry standard elements like upselling, expectations at different meals, and sidework.

ATTITUDE

If you really want to make the big money, you must learn to empathize with your customer. Give the customer the service that you would want at a restaurant. Try this, for example: The next time you go out to eat, try to see yourself from your waiter's point of view. Are you a good customer or a bad one? Are you a high-maintenance guest or an easygoing one? Then, when you become a waiter, try to remember exactly what *you* wanted from your server. Notice your own needs as a customer and turn those needs around to give them to your people. You may discover that your attitude as a patron was "I'm paying for the meal and I want it the way I want it. Period." Remember that feeling, and keep it in mind when serving the unruly customer. You know, the woman who drives you to drink by sending her steak back three times. This exercise will help you keep both your sanity and your tips.

There are many different attitudes a waiter can have toward his customers. Careless indifference is one mindset, as in "Oh, did you want something?" after they have waited ten minutes for you to happen by. Sure, the customer has been entertained while playing with the salt shaker until you finally showed up, but I'm sure he would have rather gotten the ball rolling on that meal thing he's there for. Lest you had any doubt, I do not suggest careless indifference as an outlook for the beginner waiter.

There's also utter contempt, as in "What do *you* want?" spoken while treating your tables with layered-on-disdain. But the attitude that will save your mental health and get you the furthest (at least at first) is an attitude of **helpful attentiveness**. Helpful attentiveness means a willingness to do anything that will make your customer happy during his meal. If a customer wants crêpes even though they're not on the menu, you'll check with the kitchen to see what they can whip up (chances are they'll say no, but you still win points with the guest because you tried).

If a customer is under the mistaken impression that there's alcohol in the virgin strawberry daiquiri, you'll go back to the bar and have a new one made. A lot of bartenders will just throw it back into the blender and reblend if they don't think there's anything wrong with the drink, but that's his karma to worry about. The point is that as long as the customer *feels* that you are going out of your way for his or her needs, you will rise above the rest. Helpful attentiveness is all about schmoozing.

Try not to vary your service by judging your customers on the basis of how well you think they'll tip you. Unless you have a lot of regulars (or you are psychic), you will never be able to tell who tips well and who does not. The grungy kid on the skateboard might decide to give you ten bucks because he's been a waiter once, too. Or, as it happened to me once, the guy in the tuxedo who orders two bottles of Champagne might pay the bill with crumpled singles and a handful of change, not with the crisp $100 bill like you would expect.

An interesting phenomenon may develop as you become a better waiter. As you get more skilled in anticipating your customers' needs, and less forgetful of your customers' wants, you will start to find that you don't need to be as nice as you once did. Of course, niceness is always, um, nice, but once you are meeting all your customers' expectations, you will find that you sometimes

make better tips when you're a little bit brusque with them, less chirpy, more curt. Who knows why this happens, but sometimes, customers feel like they have to live up to your expectation of them as a good customer.

Beware, however: This strategy works only if you are a good waiter. If you try to have an attitude and don't deliver the goods, you'll end up with numerous customer complaints and empty pockets.

JOB DESCRIPTION

Now that we've established the appropriate attitude for a beginning waiter, we should explore some of the different roles that you'll play in this profession.

FOOD SERVER

You take orders, you bring drinks and food. Simple, right?

ARBITER OF TASTE

Your customers will assume that you've eaten and have an opinion on everything on the menu. We know that that's not true. Some of us don't eat meat, some don't eat cheese, etc. But your customer doesn't know this. You could blatantly lie, but why?

Instead, find out people's opinions of the food you're serving. You can poll your customers, the chef, the waitstaff—anyone who eats the food. Getting secondhand info on the grub is a better path than the following example. In response to a customer's question, "Can you describe the cold meatloaf?" one waiter said, "Cold. Meat. Loaf. Anything else?" Be helpful, and your chances of making cash are that much better.

So, when a customer asks, "What's your specialty?" you will now have a response. You've learned through your own tastes and through the recommendations of others. Take this information and use it to your advantage—if something is "delicious" and more expensive than a different item, which is just as good, use your brain and recommend the more expensive item. This will increase the total bill amount, which should make your tip bigger. See the section on Upselling which starts on page 51.

INDENTURED SERVANT

When people go out to eat, they want to feel pampered and coddled for the brief time that they are in your restaurant. It is your job to do everything in your power to make them feel this way. Basically, you are their personal slave for an hour. You are the point person between the customer and everyone else who works in the restaurant. If the kitchen makes the entrées before the appetizer, it's your fault. If the food runners drop the orders at the wrong table, it's your fault. If the host seats five tables in your section at the same time, and you forget to bring one customer her soup while scrambling to get twenty drinks, it's your fault. Customers, unless they have waited tables themselves before, do not care that you have five other tables to take care of aside from theirs—they want their food, they want good service, and they want it pronto.

It is your duty to make your customers feel like you are doing everything in your power to serve them. They will (usually) forgive slow service if you smile apologetically and tell them that you're a little swamped. But if they think you are lazy, they will leave a penny on the table and complain to the manager. Jump, or at least make it look like you are jumping, when they say so. In reality, your customers are your boss: They are the ones who give you the money you walk home with at night, and they won't let you forget it, either.

STYLE POLICE

This role of the waiter varies with the restaurant you are working in, but if the place is at all upscale, the customers want to feel like fashionable, carefree, big spenders while they're in the establishment. You can help them live up to this fantasy by adding an affluent connotation to the items on the menu. For example, you could describe the hamburger with ketchup as "seared ground sirloin with a scrumptious tomato purée, seasoned with fifty-seven different spices." OK, so glamorizing ketchup is a bit of a stretch. But if you act like the place is a big deal, chances are your customers will give you a big tip to match the restaurant's ego.

Being the "style police" for your restaurant means upholding a certain standard of luxury and élan. This is another reason to suggest the more expensive things on the menu; paying more for food that you can often make better for yourself at home makes you feel wealthy. So depending on the price level and reputation of your restaurant, your customers might want to borrow some of the prestige of the restaurant for themselves during their hour at the table. Because if a restaurant is ritzy, the cus-

tomers feel ritzy. Anything you can do to help them cultivate that impression will often mean bigger tips for you.

SIDEWORK: A NECESSARY PAIN IN YOUR BUTT

Every restaurant requires all of its workers to do various
little jobs that help keep the restaurant running efficiently.
This is called sidework.

Typical sidework jobs include:

making coffee/stacking coffee cups
filling sugar dispensers/salt/pepper shakers
marrying ketchup/mustard bottles*
sweeping sections
restocking desserts
restocking plates
restocking salad and salad dressings
wiping down trays

Honestly, sidework sucks—everyone in the service
industry knows this. But, we also know that sidework is
essential to the smooth operation of a restaurant. By
ignoring or slacking on your sidework, you will hurt your
tips. When you are looking franti-
cally for milk for the coffee and
you must run all the way to the
cooler downstairs because someone forgot to stock it, you are
using up your valuable time, and
as you know, time is moolah.

* This may sound like
inter-condiment dating,
but it just means making
those odd sculptures by
balancing one ketchup
bottle on top of another
to waste as little ketchup
(or mustard or olive oil or
whatever) as possible.

You will also irritate your coworkers, who are depending on everyone to pitch in and do their fair share. So in your first few weeks at your restaurant, make sure you know what sidework is assigned to your station, and have a veteran waiter show you how to do it properly. It will save everybody time and heartache.

YOUR TYPICAL DAY

What is the typical workday like? Here's a run through.

Your shift change happens during a slow time—7 A.M., 10:30 A.M., or 4:30 P.M., for example. You punch in, look over your section to make sure all the right stuff is on the tables (correct silverware, knives facing the right way, etc.), and add things that are missing, like ketchup or salt/pepper shakers. Then check what sidework you're supposed to do.

As you do your sidework you keep an eye on your section. A loner dribbles in and sits in your section. You sigh loudly and drift over to the table. "Hi!" you chirp, with a concerned look on your face. "Has anyone taken your order yet? No? Goodness. What can I get for you?" Take his order, get his drink, bring out his appetizer, bring him a refill on his drink, bring out his food, stop by to check that everything is the way he wants it, bring him some extra salad dressing, and refill his drink again. Then you can relax and flirt with the bartender while your lone customer finishes his food. You then walk over to clear his plates, ask him if he wants dessert, bring him coffee and the check, and thank him for coming. There you go! Not too hard, huh? And when the rush hits, it's the same process as above, except multiplied by six.

When it comes close to the end of your shift, let your customers know that you'll be leaving soon. Dropping the check on their table should give them the hint that you want them to pay up. Some restaurants ask you to transfer the check if a new waiter is taking over your section, or if a table is in the middle of their meal. This is a judgment call: Do you feel you can let that tip go? Or do you have the time to hang out and wait until the table is finished? It's really up to you.

You do all of your closing sidework, reconcile your closed checks with the computer, figure out how much you made in tips, and leave.✤

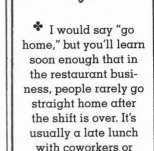

✤ I would say "go home," but you'll learn soon enough that in the restaurant business, people rarely go straight home after the shift is over. It's usually a late lunch with coworkers or shift drinks after work.

UPSELLING

Depending on the whim of the owners and managers, restaurants have different levels of importance of upselling, which I'll define as "suggesting various options to your customers in the hope that they'll buy more." In this role, the waiter is very much a salesperson, offering the customer items they did not ask for but which they decide to buy because of your well-aimed pitch. At its best, upselling is a case of a knowledgeable server's informing customers of alternatives they might enjoy. At its worst, it's an avaricious waiter preying on the weakness of his clientele, influencing them to buy things they didn't really want. Try to think of upselling in its best light, because you'll feel less sleazy. Upselling adds more money to your check. More base money spent means a bigger grand total, which should translate into bigger tips if you're doing everything else right. Don't be *too* pushy about upselling, but it is definitely a good talent to practice.

The most basic things to upsell are:

drinks
appetizers
side orders
desserts
after–dinner drinks
coffee

DRINK ORDERS

Upsell the liquor. If someone orders a vodka tonic, ask them if they want that with Absolut (or Stolichnaya, or Finlandia, depending on what call liquors your restaurant stocks).

Upselling the liquor requires knowing what liquors most basic drinks contain, and then remembering a couple of brand-name liquors in each category. The information provided in the Extras A section on page 105 can get you started memorizing drinks and alcohol brands.

FYI—upselling the liquor generally works better with a younger, more image-conscious and advertising-influenced crowd. Older people who are imbibing generally know their drink—if they want a call liquor, they'll ask for it.

FOOD ORDERS

Appetizers

Once you know what everyone wants to drink, but before they order their food, you can sometimes "get them started" with an appetizer. The best time to ask about this is right when you drop off their drinks. "Can I start you out with an appetizer?" Some sure things customers like are nachos, buffalo wings, fried calamari, or anything an entire table can pick at. Make sure your appetizers come out of the kitchen quickly; you don't want the customers waiting forever for their snack-ee-poo.

You can also try to sell appetizers just after they finish ordering their meal. Simply say, "Would you like to start off with anything? The fried cheese here is great for an app." You can also offer small house salads or soups to start with if they seem like the kind of customers who like eating lite.

Entrées

When taking entrée orders, you also have numerous opportunities to upsell: You can suggest side orders or add-ons that add to the pleasure of the meal. Again, this requires knowing the menu well and sampling food combinations yourself. It is also important to know if the kitchen gets angry when you modify entrées. Some restaurants will not let the customers make big modifications to menu items during really busy meals. But otherwise, if you know that the tomato basil pasta is absolutely delicious with grilled chicken on top of it, don't hesitate to tell your customer.

They'll end up with a better dining experience that we hope will translate into better tips for you!

DESSERTS AND AFTER-DINNER DRINKS

Your ability to sell desserts will depend, in part, on the size of the entrées at your restaurant. If people are stuffed, there's no way you'll be able to get them to order a dessert, no matter how delectable your descriptions of the chocolate mousse cake sound. If your customers seem like they are going to linger anyway, try selling them some specialty coffees, if your restaurant offers them. Irish coffee or cappuccinos with Frangelico or Bailey's are always popular. Check out page 115 for more post-dinner drink suggestions.

A sidebar: If your restaurant is busy, don't be so anxious to offer coffee and dessert. Desserts add another fifteen minutes onto a dinner, when you could have another table seated and well on their way to entréeland! The extra six to ten dollars isn't going to raise your tip as much as getting a new table in and turning, turning, turning!

Remember, every time you get a customer to buy something he didn't originally ask for, you win. But remember also that the best salesperson is a convincing one—you can't consistently sell your customers something you don't believe in. So don't try to pass off the fried mozzarella sticks as scrumptious when you really think they taste like breaded caulking glue. You won't look like a stellar waiter when your customer can't stand them either! Your conviction in a dish's deliciousness will really be the ultimate selling tool.

THE DIFFERENT MEALS AND
HOW TO TREAT THEM

Each meal has a different, ahem, flavor, and knowing what to expect while serving these meals will help you prepare for each one.

BREAKFAST

Coffee. Coffee. Coffee. Make sure that you have a warmer ready with plenty of java, because in the morning, people want their caffeine. Don't provoke the early morning anger of grumpy addicts by neglecting to refill their bottomless cups.

Breakfast is a pretty easy, but unfortunately not very lucrative, meal. Items on the menu for breakfast are generally pretty cheap, and most people don't start with appetizers. So unless you're working at a restaurant that specializes in caviar omelets, you're going to be disappointed with fifteen percent of your checks. But buck up: lunch, with its automatic high turnover, is on the way.

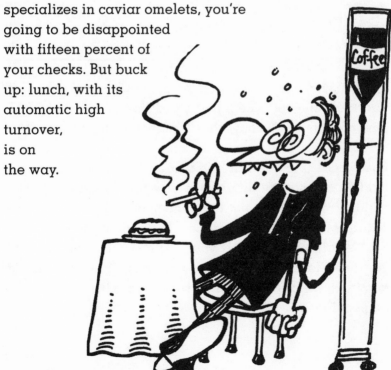

LUNCH

People often have a tight schedule for this meal, especially during the week, and anything you can do to help them keep within their time requirements is a bonus on your part. This time pressure is the best thing about the lunchtime crowd—your tables turn themselves automatically, without your worrying about using the tricks you'll soon learn to force people out! Again though, lunch isn't really where the big bucks are . . . dinner is your gravy train.

DINNER

This meal can make you a lot of money if you're smart. People out to dinner are more likely to buy drinks, and more food, and you should take this opportunity to upsell like a madman. The dinner crowd is more likely to be receptive to your suggestions, because often they're out for entertainment as well as just a meal. This is where your role as the arbiter of taste comes in—make people feel rich and care-free by selling them bottled water and name-brand liquors. You will develop sensors very quickly—these sensors will tell you what customers not to bother upselling to at dinner. These are the customers that you'd like to be rid of ASAP (and of course, you know, they'll probably stay all night).

Each meal is inherently the same ("Hi there, want some food?"), only with different elements emphasized. The meal, however, does not have the most influence over the quality of your work experience: The people you work with do. Certain people affect your life more than others, and you need to make an effort to cultivate friendships and goodwill, which conveniently brings us to the next section on people.

WORKING WITH PEOPLE

YOU ARE THE LINCHPIN in the relationship between the customer and the restaurant, but there are also plenty of behind-the-scenes players. It's not you doing the cooking, right?

So it takes a lot of people to make a restaurant run, and the following section will clue you in on the individuals who help make your job easier.

YOUR MANAGER

Although it may seem obvious that you must get on your manager's good side, there are some finer points you should be aware of. Your real "boss" is the customer, and you should definitely make a point of schmoozing the person who actually puts cash tips in your pocket. However, it is important for anyone on any level in the service industry to manage their relationship with their manager.

The manager of the restaurant is god. Your god. Even if you can't stand this person, you must kiss serious butt. This person makes your schedule, assigns your section of tables, cleans up your mistakes, helps you cover your shifts when you can't make it to the restaurant, and basically rules your life when you are at work. And, since absolute power corrupts absolutely, if you don't get on your manager's good side, you will be crushed. Try to pick a restaurant with a good management team, as I mentioned in the last chapter. And work hard to please the manager—it will only pay off.

WHEN YOU FIRST START WORK, MANAGE EXPECTATIONS AND GET A STAR REPUTATION

An old recipe for success says: Work hard, and make sure your managers think you're working harder. This applies to any job that you may have, but be sure not to forget it while waiting tables.

There is no need to brag about your table service savvy. Keep your boss's expectations low, so you can blow those expectations right out of the water. The helpful hints contained in this book can help you do just that! Let your work speak for you, and your manager will be much more impressed at the job you're doing. Show your managers that you're a sensational worker from day one: Get on their good side. There is absolutely nothing a manager likes more than to know that a server is trying his or her best.

WORK YOUR BUTT OFF FOR THE FIRST FOUR WEEKS

As I just said, managers love seeing that an employee is really trying. All you have to do when you start is be flexible. If for your first couple of weeks you are the person who offers to stay late or pick up the bad shifts (or any shifts), your managers will notice. By staying late, you'll have a little more time to get to know the managers (yes, schmoozing allowed), and you'll be helping them out. They won't forget it. You can also reap benefits from working like a machine for those initial thirty days. If you can establish yourself as a "helper" in this time period, you won't have to work nearly as hard after that first month. Your reputation as a stud worker is established. By that same token, a reputation as a slacker will stick for the duration of your employment at that restaurant. Why do that when it's so easily avoidable?

BE FLEXIBLE AND WILLING

Try to be as helpful and easygoing with the managers as you are with your customers.✤ At first, you are going to get the dog shifts, and you might even have to work in the kitchen, or be a busboy for a while before you start waiting tables. But if you cheerfully accept these bad assign-

---

✤ Even though you should have a great attitude about anything that management lets you do, whether it be hosting, food running, bussing tables, etc., don't let yourself get caught in that job. Waiting tables is where the money is, and that's where you want to be. Make sure your manager gives you a date for when you can start training for your table service position, and follow up on that date.

ments and then do well in them, your manager will be much more receptive to giving you the good shifts. When you're new at a restaurant, you don't have any credits to use as leverage toward getting what you want. But, after a few weeks of an ungrudging attitude and hard work, you will have garnered that star reputation that will allow you to make more demands of your managers. A good attitude can go a long way with both the managers and the customers. So, start off strong, and be flexible.

HOW TO SCHMOOZE YOUR MANAGER WHILE WORKING YOUR SHIFTS

The least amount of trouble you make for your manager, the better. Let's try to understand the manager's mentality. He has limited time. The requests that waiters make are completely random, just like your customers' requests of you. So, the less of your manager's time you take up, the better. The more problems you have that need a manager's help, whether it's about food returns, mistakes, or schedule changes, the more likely the boss is going to brand you as a troublemaker.

THEREFORE, TRY TO BE UNOBTRUSIVE

Don't run to the manager with every little mistake you make. First ask one of the veteran waiters what to do and they can advise you whether it's worth bothering a manager. Most mistakes are not, so ask first. If you *do* have to get a manager to fix your mistake, *don't lie* to make yourself look better (like pretending that your customers changed their minds from cheesecake to French toast when in fact those buttons are right next to each other on the computer and your finger slipped). Everyone makes mistakes, and managers expect them from both staff who are new to the service industry and veteran waiters new to a job. An honest employee who screws up every now and then is a lot more valuable than a shady employee who never bugs the managers but seems dishonest. This does not mean that every time you've made an itty-bitty glitch you should run to the manager since "honesty is the best policy." Honesty doesn't mean spill your guts every time something goes wrong. You'll seem incompetent. But, when you need help and veteran waiters can't fix the problem, go to a manager and be honest. You'll gain more points for your honesty, and, seriously, everyone makes mistakes.

So, if you manage your manager's expectations of you, don't make yourself look inept, and tell the truth when you've made a mistake, your manager will be tickled pink with you. You may even get some schmooze points out of the situation.

DEALING WITH YOUR MANAGER: COVER YOUR SHIFTS

You are responsible for your scheduled shifts. If you can't make it to one of your shifts, do everything in your power to find yourself a replacement. Only call in sick when you really are sick, not when it's a beach day and you want to go bake. Beach days come and go—good jobs do not. You will also irritate your fellow employees by calling in sick if you aren't. They will find out, and they will be angry that they got called in on their day off (when, just like you, they really wanted to be at the beach). You also risk irritating your manager, whom you worked so hard to be best buds with. They, while dealing with all the other restaurant crap, must make phone calls to find someone to fill in for you. So, do your own legwork to cover your shifts, and show your manager what a responsible, hardworking individual you are.

ASK FOR HELP!

If you get slammed and you can't handle your tables, TELL someone. Don't try to hide it in the vain and futile hope that you'll be able to deal with the nightmare on your own. You won't.

So at that point, ask for help. The cavalry can be a veteran waiter who looks bored, a lingering busboy, or even your manager. But if you try to handle a sticky, busy situation on your own, you may end up screwing up in a major way. Although it might seem counterintuitive to tell your manager when your workload is too heavy, most managers would prefer your coming to them early when you can't handle your tables to your coming when it's too late and you've put in the wrong orders for everyone and can't remember who gets what. Just take a deep breath, and ask for help. It's really much easier than cleaning up the mess you'll create if you don't ask for help.

To get on your manager's good side, do your best to make yourself seem in control and capable, rather than needy and clueless. A big part of being in control and capable is knowing when to ask for help if you need it.

OTHER PEOPLE TO SCHMOOZE INCLUDE:

THE BUSBOYS

Supposedly, the main job of the busboy is just to clear tables and occasionally refill water glasses. But, if you pick a couple of favorites and tip them a few dollars more, they'll help you take care of your customers when you're busy. A busboy will get water and silverware and even food orders for you if you're nice to him, which makes your job easier and keeps your customers happy. Busboys can help you turn your tables more quickly, meaning more money for you at the end of the night. If the busboys don't like you, however, you may find yourself clearing your own tables. Treat them nice, they'll treat you nice.

THE BARTENDERS

A bartender can make your life hell if he dislikes you. He can prepare your drinks slowly, which will annoy your customers and waste your time. So never skimp on tipping out the bartender, and thank that person profusely, even if you think he's lazy.

VETERAN WAITERS

It will be very obvious to you who the long-term waiters at your restaurant are: They're the ones who get all the good shifts, who can take off for two weeks during the busy season, and who treat you like dirt because they've seen hundreds of new waiters come and go through the place. If you can get in good with a couple of the old-timers, you'll have a friend to turn to. This friend can tell you which managers to avoid, what are good shifts to get, shortcuts in the restaurant, and they won't get annoyed when you need to find out what's in the Middle Eastern Combo. Old waiters can also cover your butt when you screw up, and help you cover your tables when you're swamped.

The easiest way to make friends with the veteran waiters is to help them out when they're busy and you're not, like getting water for a table, or taking an order. Believe me, there will be many times when you first start out when they'll be busy and you won't, since they will have the good sections, and you'll have the dogs. You might as well make that time worth something. I would advise, however, to either ask them if they need your help, or let them know what you are doing to help them. You don't want to seem like you are doing things behind their back, well-intentioned or not.

Your best way to become comfortable in the restaurant is to make friends with everyone. Let people know you are there to help and work hard, and soon the other kids will let you play with them, too. The coworkers you meet while waiting tables can be some of the best people you'll know. Be yourself and give your all, and your experience will be the best you can have!

POLITICS

Every organization of people has its own politics, and restaurants are by no means immune. There will always be cliques, and managers will always have favorites. If you're well liked, or at least harmless, you will be able to come in, work, and make your money in peace. If, however, you don't get along with other workers, you will find yourself miserable at work. Try to be nice, friendly, and helpful, at least for the first few weeks. Be helpful to other people, and please, think twice before you "fish off the work pier" by fooling around with a coworker. Rumors fly in the service industry, and people *love* to talk. So try to be bland, at least at first. Once you've established what a superb waiter you are, and how helpful you can be, you can let the beast show a little. But watch your back: Politics is a powerful thing.

BIG TIPS ON MAKIN' BIG TIPS

WHAT IS IT ABOUT THOSE OLD WAITERS that lets them make so much money so effortlessly? This chapter contains some of the techniques that separate the veteran waiters from the amateurs.

This is what you need to know to be a good waiter.

1
TREAT YOUR SECTION LIKE ONE BIG TABLE

The better you are at assessing the needs of *all* your customers at the same time, the more efficient you'll be as a waiter, saving yourself both time and sanity. Seeing your entire section as one table means making your rounds to each group and anticipating what your customers want before they even have to ask for it. So, if one table motions you over to ask you for more napkins, check around to all your other tables to see if they need anything. Always check people's drink levels, so you can gauge if they'll want a refill. (The most annoying thing a waiter can encounter is getting a drink for one person at a table and having two more people at the table ask for drinks while you're dropping off the first. If you didn't say, "Would anyone else like something from the bar?"

then it's really your own fault that you're doing all that extra work.)

If you are able to effectively foresee what your tables need, you can prevent yourself from running around like crazy at the whim of every customer. Cover all your bases while you're dealing with a table, and check all your tables at the same time, rather than going back and forth. This is the most helpful hint a new waiter can learn. Work on developing this skill.

2
ACKNOWLEDGE YOUR TABLES AS SOON AS THEY SIT DOWN, AND BE CONSTANTLY IN THEIR FIELD OF VISION

Never, EVER ignore your tables unless you really don't feel like making money. Even if you're totally in the weeds and won't be able to take their order for half an hour, you should *always* let your customers know that you know they are there. Customers get very annoyed if they feel like they are being ignored. So, acknowledge them when they sit down by saying something like, "Hi there! I'll be with you in just a moment." And, after you've said hello, if you really don't have time to get to them, make sure a busboy gives them water (bread also, if it's served in your restaurant), and get another waiter to take their drink order.

Now it sometimes happens that you don't even have time to get to the table to say hello. Try this: When you finally get a spare moment to get to their table, pretend it's not your section, and that you're just a helpful coworker of their deficient serv-

er, and you're concerned that they haven't been
helped. Say, with a frown of worry on your face,
"Has anyone come by to take your order yet? No?
Oh, I'm so sorry! Let me take care of you. What
can I getcha?" They will be so grateful that
someone actually came to check on them that
they'll practically throw money at you.

While customers are sitting in your section, try
to make yourself readily available to act on
their slightest whim. Customers want accessi-
bility to their server. They want you to be ever-present in
your section, catering to everything they desire. We know
that's not possible, but if you can make them believe that
you're always around, you've won! To accomplish this,
simply hang around where your customers can see you or
where you can see them craning their necks to see you.
Try not to disappear for extended periods of time. This
ever-present hovering makes your clients happy. It may
be irritating to you, but you're at work to make money, and
the more attention you pay to your customers' needs, the
more you will make.

3
TAKE CARE OF CUSTOMERS'
RANDOM UNSCHEDULED DEMANDS

The reason you're ever-present in your station is so that
when one of your tables asks you for more ketchup (or
napkins, or water, or anything else when you're not
expecting it), you can do this for them right away. You
must do it right away because, unless you have an ele-
phantine memory, you will forget to do it. Forgetfulness
annoys customers to no end. They think to themselves, "I

told her expressly that I wanted more powdered sugar! She hasn't brought it because she wants to teach me a lesson for asking them to heat my maple syrup. How dare she? Ooh, and now my French toast is cold. I think I'll leave a nasty note on the table instead of a tip." Believe me, things like this do go through their minds. Avoid this situation. At least avoid looking like an idiot when you go around to their table and brightly ask them if they need anything, and they say, "Yeah, another Coke, remember?" Take care of the customers as soon as they ask. Because chances are that every minute they don't have what they want, they're sitting there drumming their fingers on the table and convincing themselves how bad their meal is without it.

4
DON'T GET STUCK AT ONE TABLE WHEN YOU HAVE OTHER TABLES CLAMORING FOR YOUR ATTENTION

Sometimes customers will slow you down because they're not ready to order, and they want to ask you a ton of questions. This is just fine when you have all the time in the world because your section is empty or you're all caught up. But if table 25 wants their check, and rowdy table 20 needs their drink refills, every minute you spend on the wishy-washy couple at table 23 is money out of your pockets.

I'm not advocating rudeness to customers who don't know what they want, and I'm certainly not saying not to be helpful (it's the perfect opportunity to upsell an expensive entrée). However, when you are super-busy and don't have time to spare even for upselling, you must firmly tell your customer that you'll give her a little more time with the menu. Chances are, the indecisive person has heard this before.

5
KEEPING CALM

Even if all your customers want to make substitutions that aren't programmed into the computer or they all have a plane to catch in five minutes, try to seem calm. A flustered, harried waiter is unattractive. And, your calm image will help to calm the crazy customer—as long as they *think* everything is under control. Therefore, anything you can do to generate an aura of control will be to your benefit, even if the computer system has broken down and the kitchen has lost all your orders. This might mean freshening up your makeup, having a cigarette, or complaining to a coworker. Whatever it is, figure out early what will keep you chipper while working your shifts. You'll need it.

When you're really busy, really in the weeds, and you feel like you're about to go crazy, take a deep breath and be calm. Think Zen. Then take the next step and prioritize. Group similar tasks together, and try to get them done as fast as you can. For example, get the drinks for all your tables at the same

IN THE WEEDS

time rather than running back and forth to the bar. But you're only human. If you try to rush things too much, you'll end up making mistakes, which will slow you down a lot in the long run when you have to correct them.

Also, if you're really slammed, you're probably not the only one. If you're really busy, the kitchen is busy, the bar is busy, the managers are busy, and so are your coworkers. So, when you screw up, you're slowing down not only yourself but also everyone else, and they're just as weeded as you are. So even though you feel like screaming like a hyena and bringing your tables whatever orders happen to be ready when you're in the kitchen, just stay calm and conquer your tasks in an orderly fashion.

This frantic restaurant time gives you a great opportunity to gauge whom you can call your friend. In one restaurant, when the waitstaff was slammed and the kitchen wasn't, the cooks made food for their favorite waiters first, poured soup into bowls for them, and even put the food on trays for the harried waiters. Help like that is what can get you through a crazy shift.

6
CLEAR YOUR TABLES

When your customer puts his knife and fork side-by-side on his plate, pushes his plate away, or leans back with his arms crossed, he is ready for his finished dishes to be taken away. Customers get annoyed when their dirty plates stay on their table for too long, reminding them of their gluttony. Don't rely too heavily on the busboys to notice this before you do; keep your eyes on your section and what's going on. The faster you clear a table, the faster you will turn that table. Be conscious of your section and clear the table if a dirty plate is staring at you.

7
TIMING

There are times when it is crucial that you perform certain tasks for your customers, and other periods when you can sit back and relax for a while. Here are some crucial times when you need to be on the ball:

When your customer sits down

Get your booty over there and say hello ASAP, like we talked about earlier.

After you get their drink orders

Hustle to bring them their beverage. If you are too busy to make it to the bar and back, then get a busboy to bring them bread and water. Like prison inmates, customers can be sustained for quite some time if they've got these two staples. But if they don't have anything to toy with at the table, they can get testy.

If they have their drinks and they're browsing the menu, you may be able relax a bit. It depends on how they look vis á vis their menus. Are the menus open or closed? Are your customers in the midst of a conversation you don't want to interrupt or are they looking at you, ready to order? (Most breakfast/lunch diners will definitely want to order when you return with their drinks. Dinner customers usually take more time with the menu.)

Here are the times when you can take it easy, or focus on your other new tables to begin the whole cycle again:

After they order their dinner

Customers don't mind waiting about ten or fifteen minutes for their main course, or longer if they had an appetizer, salad, or a bread basket.

Dessert and coffee time

Let 'em linger over their french roast, if you're weeded with your other tables.

When they're done

Drop the check when it's convenient for you. They won't get *too* upset if you make them wait.

Once you gain experience, you can begin to play with the timing. For example, if you have a particularly busy section and you don't want to seat another table until you're ready to do all that rushing around discussed above, you can hold onto the table's check a bit longer until you're ready to let them go.

You are in control of the timing of your customers' meals. If you need some extra time to do something, or to catch up, you can hold off putting in a table's dinner order . . . you can be your customers' food and drink god! I think I like that idea.

8
DON'T WASTE A TRIP

If you go to a table empty-handed or leave empty-handed, you're wasting a trip. This means that when you approach a table, perhaps you should be bringing more water or extra napkins. But more importantly, when you leave that table, you should bring one of their used glasses or their empty bread basket back with you. As frequently mentioned, the more you can keep in control of your own time and minimize your tasks, the more efficient you will become. By keeping on top of your tables you'll make your job easier. For example, hot entrées come out of the kitchen and the customers' salad dishes are still on the tables. You could have removed them from the table when you brought the second round of drinks! "Not wasting a trip" is a good thing to keep in mind, although in practice it can be hard to implement. But if a little alarm bell goes off in your head asking you what you're bringing to or taking from the table each time, you will be increasing your efficiency.

9
KEEP UPDATED CHECKS WITH YOU, READY TO BE DROPPED ON YOUR TABLES

Some waiters like to print out their checks each time they ring a new order so that they have them ready to give to the customer. (Some computer systems print out new checks automatically.) If your restaurant uses handwritten duplicate checks (a.k.a. dupes), try to gauge whether your customers will be ordering anything else, and tally their total when you have a spare minute, before they ask you for the check. Keeping your customers' checks with you can save you time when you're busy: It puts you less at the mercy of the customers' immediate needs and more in control of your own time, which is the point, right? Having updated checks with you can prevent too many empty-handed trips back and forth from the computer, thereby leaving your customer to control your time. If you keep updated checks with you, you'll be able to exercise more control over your tables.

10
WHEN YOU FINALLY START GETTING THE GOOD STATIONS, COME IN EARLY

It is amazing how much of a difference ten minutes makes to the quality of your service and the abundance of your tips in a busy restaurant. When you arrive early to work, you have time to survey your station, check all the important sidework and do it, find out the specials and the soup of the day, and talk to the waiter who had the station before you to find out if you're getting any transferred tables. If, on the other hand, you're late, you'll be running to play catch-up with yourself for at least an hour. You won't have time to give your first customers that extra attention they crave, and you will feel this in your tips.

11
TURNING YOUR TABLES—TRICKS TO GET PEOPLE TO LEAVE YOUR STATION

When a guest has overstayed his welcome at your house, there are a number of signs that you give him to let him know his time in your home is up. You could inquire about when he needs his ride to the airport, or you could pack his clothes for him.

Unfortunately, we must be a bit more subtle in the service industry, but there are ways to be rid of customers who are taking up prime real estate in your section. If they're not paying for their property, you can ease them to the door. Here are the top five—I'm sure there are many, many more.

1. Keep picking up the check, as if you are looking for money or a credit card under it. This works best if your restaurant has check "books" that the check goes inside.
2. Start clearing everything off the table including their unfinished drinks, and wiping it down in front of them so that they have trouble keeping up their conversation. (You can only do this after they've paid the check, or else there goes your tip.)
3. Ask, "I'm sorry, did you need change?" when they have yet to put any money on the table. You can also tell them what credit cards your restaurant accepts.
4. Stand next to the table with your arms crossed and your lips pursed. You can also do this a little more subtly by lingering around the table and glancing repeatedly at the check.
5. If you have some truly stubborn tables, just ask the host to subtly change the music. No, it doesn't matter what you change the music to, as long as it is a somewhat different style from the preceding selection. So follow John Coltrane with Bach, and you'll watch people fly out of your section. This is the most bizarre phennomenon, but it works wonders in Grendel's Den in Cambridge.

KEY SKILLS

THE SKILLS THAT I'VE CHOSEN to cover in this chapter are the skills that a waiter at *any* level should have. These skills are second nature to the experienced waiter, and should become second nature to the inexperienced waiter. They are:

Knowing the items on the menu
Learning to carry many things at a time
Improving your short-term memory
Making small talk

MEMORIZING THE MENU

One of the most useful things you can do is learn your restaurant's menu by heart. Most restaurants will make you learn it anyway by giving you a pop quiz, but it's for a reason. When the customer inquires about the Silver City soup, you can reel off the top four ingredients quickly. Customers expect you to be familiar with your restaurant's menu. You are not doing them a favor by knowing the menu—it's part of your job. If you don't know the menu, you'll waste time and look like a doodad if you have to say, "Um wait, let me go ask the kitchen what bruschetta is."

After working at the restaurant for a month or so, you will have inadvertently learned most of the menu, but the earlier you do it, the quicker you'll be on your way to satisfying the customer and making the dinero.

There are certain things you should be able to point out on the menu aside from the most tasty dishes: low-fat, low-calorie meals, anything for people watching their sodium or dairy intake, light nibbling dishes, and food for children. These are the most common special items that people ask for, so be prepared in advance to answer these questions. Turkey sandwiches and turkey or veggie burgers tend to be good for dieters, pastas for restricted dieters, chips and salsa for munching, hot dogs, chicken fingers, or fries for children. Also, have a few of your own favorites, or, to add a little flair, "house specialties" that you can offer your customer. Have one fave food for each course (appetizer, entrée, and dessert). But don't embarrass yourself with your suggestion—you don't want to suggest fried mushrooms as the chef's specialty when you know they come out burnt half the time!

ON MAKING RECOMMENDATIONS

The customer will ask you whether a specific menu item is good. Unless it really sucks, you should always say it's delicious. In fact, it's one of your favorite things on the menu. Why? Because the customer obviously wants to order that item, but for some reason needs some confirmation in making that decision. Hold your customer's hand. Reaffirm their self-esteem. Tell them they've made a brilliant choice. Don't bother suggesting something else at that point, because they won't order it. When they ask you about the sloppy Joes, they already know they want it, they just need a little push. So give 'em a nudge and tell them it's terrific, and how clever they are to order it. A little ego stroking of a client never hurt anyone's bottom line.

Don't tell a customer he's making the right choice if he is ordering the worst thing on the menu, though. If they ask you about the gluey gazpacho, don't tell them it's great or the customer might send it back, and you'll look like a liar. If the thing they ask about is really yucky, either keep quiet or tell them it bites. They'll get it anyway, then gag on it and agree with you, and tip you while saying that they shoulda listened. Hello, cash in your pockets!

CARRYING MANY THINGS AT ONE TIME
(WITHOUT DROPPING THEM)

Knowing how to juggle two soups and a couple of drinks will save you a lot of time while you're running around trying to please your customers. Since the rules and formats of each restaurant will affect just what you'll be carrying, the best way to pick up this skill is to actively observe or even take lessons from the veteran waitstaff at your restaurant. They can show you the tricks of how to carry three coffee cups in one hand. It takes practice, but it's really not that hard. This is yet another reason to get cozy with the more tenured waiters at your place of employment. You can also, check page 118 for more tips on how to carry a tray.

There's a restaurant in Boston that won't let you carry food and drinks on the same tray. Why? No one knows. If you can figure out why this makes sense, drop me a line.

IMPROVING YOUR SHORT-TERM MEMORY

Although most restaurants will provide you with a pad for taking orders, your job as a waiter will be greatly enhanced if you can remember people's choices without writing them down. You will not always have an opportunity to write down everything that people want, since customers often don't care whether you have a pen in hand when they bark out their drink and food orders. A good way to start the memory process is to remember who ordered first at the table, then get the group to order in a circle clockwise from her. Most customers will let you do this, and then when you enter the check into the computer your orders will be in order!

HOW TO IMPROVE YOUR SHORT-TERM MEMORY

First, familiarity with the menu is invaluable. If you can picture each thing your customer asks for as it appears on the menu, or better yet, if you can visualize the order as you will punch it into the computer, you're well on your way to improving your short-term memory.

Another simple exercise is to repeat back the order to each customer both after the individual has ordered and after the entire table has ordered. Here's an example:

> **CUSTOMER #1:** *I'll have the Caesar salad with grilled chicken.*
> **YOU:** *Chick Caesar. Want a side of fries? No? Okay, Sir?*
> **CUSTOMER #2:** *I'll have ravioli, but with alfredo sauce, not marinara.*
> **YOU:** *Ravioli with alfredo. Care for a house salad? No? Fine. Next?* [looking expectantly at the final customer, who is perusing the menu as if it's the first published copy of the Dead Sea Scrolls.]

> **CUSTOMER #3:** *I'll take, hmm, how's the chicken Kiev? Oh, it's your favorite dish? Great! I'll take it, but with no sauce, and with butternut squash on the side instead of Brussels sprouts.*
>
> **YOU:** *Kiev, no sauce, squash. Okay, let me make sure I've got this right. Ma'am, you'd like the chicken Caesar, sir, the ravioli, but with alfredo, not marinara, and finally a chicken Kiev with no sauce, no Brussels sprouts, but with butternut squash. Okay? Anyone want a refill on drinks?*

Then you rush off to your computer to put the order in. Don't dillydally between the time that you take their order and the time that you enter it in. You don't want to end up back at the table saying, "Um, you wanted asparagus, right?" Put your order in right after you get it.

A good short-term memory will also help you keep track of your tables, so that you'll remember that the brown liquid at the bottom of a customer's glass is Bacardi and Coke and not iced coffee. Then you can politely ask if they want another one. You'll find a good short-term memory serving you well in a myriad of other situations as well, like remembering phone numbers and the name of the bar where you'll meet your friends for a well-deserved and much-needed drink when you get off work.

MAKING SMALL TALK

Knowing how to chat up your tables will directly improve your tip-ability. Some of the important small talk topics you should know, especially if you are working in a resort town, are some of the area's hot spots and important sights. If you don't frequent local bars, nightclubs, or restaurants ask other waiters for the names and addresses of a couple, so that when your party-hardy customers want to know where to hang, you can tell them.

Of course, you may find that making small talk with some of your customers is the absolute last thing you feel like doing, but strangers appreciate help and will show their appreciation. You should, however, know the boundaries of small talk with customers—if you begin to feel uncomfortable, you can tell your manager.

Small talk is about making your customers feel at home and special, as if they are more than just customers to you—special guests—friends, even. Small talk is about making a connection with the people you're waiting on. It's good for your tips, but it's also good for your soul to genuinely care about the people who are paying you. So comment on her scarf if you like it. Ask them how their day is going. Google at their baby. Flirt. You can always talk about the weather. Anything that makes them feel comfortable and pampered and special. They'll feel good, and they'll want to make you feel good, too, with cash! Ask the old-time waiters how they work their tables small-talk-wise to make tips. Try it. Small talk makes the difference between fifteen percent verses the twenty percent you deserve. Work those tables, you happy-go-lucky waiter, you!

CLIENT SERVER

THE CUSTOMER IS YOUR BOSS. This chapter tells you how to keep the boss happy, with a list of customer likes and dislikes, and various tips for dealing with them.

The following is based on a survey conducted by the National Restaurant Association on the likes, dislikes, and expectations of restaurant patrons. Read it and weep.

What do customers expect from waiters when dining out?

1. A smile and an attitude that puts customers at ease.
2. Attentiveness: where the waiter inquires whether the meal is satisfactory, or if more items or service are needed.
3. An honest estimate of how long before the meal will be served.
4. Familiarity with the menu and with how food and drinks are prepared.
5. Friendly greetings and a "thank-you" to the customer when they leave.

The Top Ten pet peeves of restaurant customers are:

1. Slow service
2. Poor service
3. Smokers around the tables
4. Food that is not fresh
5. Food served cold
6. Unsanitary conditions
7. Needlessly noisy conditions
8. Inattentive service
9. Food served incorrectly
10. Feeling as if the server is doing them a favor by waiting on them.

EVALUATE YOUR CUSTOMERS

The best waiters can look at the people sitting in their section and vary the service accordingly. This does not mean that they give bad service to people who look cheap, and good service to potential tycoons, but they can tell whether people need or want a solicitous waiter, a playful and campy one, or an extremely professional one. If you learn to anticipate the kind of service your customers want, you will make your job easier. Here are some guidelines:

1) **Senior citizens** are generally very picky. They want a server who is friendly and very deferential to their needs. Prepare to spend some time with a table of golden-agers. You'll have to patiently answer the most seemingly unimportant of questions, and record every little request. It will take you a lot of time. Expect it. Don't get bitter—this is part of your job.

2) **Businesspeople**, especially those who are having a "power lunch" where they're making deals, do not want to be unduly disturbed by the presence of the waiter's person-

ality. They do want the check and other amenities in a timely fashion. These tables require mucho attention, but attention from afar—a good waiter will keep his eye on the table to refill drinks before being asked or drop a check before the thought of paying is even a post-operative gleam in the bigwig's eye. Disturbing businesspeople while they're wheeling and dealing will lead them to snarl at you and leave a small tip. Be effortlessly efficient with them.

3) **Couples**. Your good eye must come into play when you serve couples. If it's a first date, try to keep your personality under wraps—but a couple that's obviously a couple is fair game. Be yourself and have fun. Treat a dating couple (you know, the two of them don't really look like they're "together" yet) like the businesspeople, since neither group wants to be disturbed. The personality of their waiter is often the least important thing to daters as they gaze across the garbanzo beans into each others' eyes. But, unlike with the businesspeople, you can be a little more friendly in the few brief times when they do come up for air to recognize your presence.

4) **Single Diners**. Again, a judgment call. Some single diners want to be left alone, while others may be uncomfortable by themselves or lonely. Then there are those who, it seems, are dining out for the express purpose of chatting with everyone. Loners tend to eat and run, leaving your section quickly with a big tip in their wake. Fast turnover and good money—you can't lose!

5) **Never assume that the man is paying.** In this enlightened age where eleven year olds carry their mom's gold card around with them, going dutch is a norm, and women taking men out is finally acceptable. You never know who might be paying. Don't anger the female customer by handing the check to the man. It's not politically correct, or correct in any form of the word. Better to err on the safe side by leaving the check in the middle of the table, and let them arm wrestle over who has to pay.

OBNOXIOUS CUSTOMERS

You *will* get jerks in your section. They *will* find fault with everything you do, no matter how hard you bust your butt to give them good service. It's a fact of life, it's a fact of waiting tables. You can always ask someone else to finish up the table for you, but why chicken out? Difficult people exist, and the faster you learn to deal with it, the better.

If waiting tables teaches you anything, it should be to take personally *nothing* that your customers might say. This is a good guideline for life in general, but it's much easier said than done. Complete strangers, or even casual acquaintances, really know nothing about the *real* you. They know only what they see from your actions or appearance. If they come to a conclusion about you, it probably has more to do with their own hang-ups than it does with you and your worth as a person. So, when you have difficult customers who insult you or try to pick a fight with you, they are reflecting their own problems, rather than making any valid comment about you or your ability.

Following is an excerpt from a waitstaff manual where one manager gives advice on how to handle problem customers:

*We have heard the statement "The customer is always right" many times. But is the customer always right? Sometimes they make unfair demands, or they blame the server for something out of that person's control. So first understand that **no one** is always right, including the customer. Here is another way to look at the issue: Customers may not always be right, but they are always customers, and it is okay for customers to be wrong.*

The key to the situation is to overcome the complaint, and make the customer feel that you did everything possible to solve the problem. Customers who had problems but had those problems satisfactorily resolved will become very loyal patrons, even more loyal than some clients who never had any problems in the first place! Thus, the challenge is to handle the situation so that the customer wins, whether he is right or not. ✤

When a complaint deals with something out of your direct control, like cold or incorrectly prepared food, you can be very sympathetic with the guest, fix the problem quickly, and subsequently ingratiate yourself with them. But, if the customer has a problem with you, I suggest you take it more seriously. Gauge the gravity of the customer's problem with you and if it gets out of hand, seek help and advice from management or other waitstaff.

If the customer's problem with your service is minor, you may want to go for the sympathy plug. "Sorry for the problems—it's my first week and I'm still learning the

---

✤ Excerpted from the waitstaff manual of the News Café in Miami Beach, by permission of the author, Tony Puche.

ropes." Chances are, this will calm your customer and boost your tip back up. But if things get scary, you do have other outlets to turn to for support, like your manager, the white knight, or another waiter who can take over the table.

CIRCLE TEN:
THE INSOLENT DINER

I Didn't pay attention during recitation of specials.

II. Complained to manager because waiter "didn't smile much."

III. Ordered items never seen on any menu anywhere.

IV Finger snappers/ frantic wavers

V. Walked out on check

VI Bad tippers

THE LESSER KNOWN REALM OF DANTE'S INFERNO.

PART IV
POTENTIAL PROBLEMS

WAITERS ARE A DISPOSABLE COMMODITY—there are tons out there, and every waiter is replaceable. You can choose from a plethora of ways to lose your job at a restaurant, and since there are ten waiters who would step into your job tomorrow, managers don't hesitate to fire. The following sections reveal some of the major reasons firing occurs in the service industry. You can avoid these pitfalls until you're ready to give your two weeks' notice.

AVOIDING THE FIRING SQUAD

1
DISHONESTY

In most places, you will immediately lose your job if you are caught stealing. Stealing from your restaurant can consist of taking food that you didn't pay for or charging customers for food without ringing it up, putting the money directly into your tips instead. Stealing is not worth it. Let's think about it. What is more valuable, the hamburger you crave, or your job? You may get away with it for a while, but you will eventually be found out and summarily fired. And I haven't even mentioned the karmic debt you've accumulated. Let's also remember . . . stealing is illegal.

2
INAPPROPRIATE BEHAVIOR

Coming to work drunk or under the influence of any illegal drug can get you fired very quickly. Most restaurants will also let employees go for performing intimate acts with other people in the lavatories (this happens!), drinking on the job, using or selling drugs on the premises of the restaurant, etc. It's just like high school—if your principal wouldn't let you do it, neither will your manager.

3
INSUBORDINATION

Talking back to your manager, repeatedly flouting company policy (like refusing to wear or iron your uniform), or bad-mouthing management to other waiters, are things that will mean the unemployment line for you if you keep getting caught.

4
LAZINESS

If you shirk on your assigned sidework, consistently ignore your tables' needs, are always late or not a "team player," you could be headed for the highway.

5
EXTREME INCOMPETENCE

When you've been training for over two months and the usual learning curve is five minutes, your manager may decide that they've wasted too much time and energy on you. It is rare that anyone is so incapable of doing the job that they get fired for their inability, but it does happen. Managers usually give new staff the benefit of the doubt at least until it becomes obvious that the restaurant is not benefiting from their employment.

6
SERVING ALCOHOL TO MINORS
THIS IS ILLEGAL!!

Not only will you get fired doing this but you can also get your restaurant shut down by the DEA for giving booze to tots. You can also get arrested and thrown into jail in some states. At a minimum, you'll be fined.

To avoid this fiasco, card anyone who looks younger than thirty. In fact, if you keep to this rule, you can flatter many of your customers at the same time. You may feel like the bad guy, and you may empathize with your customers when they don't have ID, but you are not there to be their friend. Most people remember to bring ID out with them, but if they don't, it's their tough luck. You must take this attitude. Personally, I would rather have the guy from table 32 drink Coke while his friends swill beer, than force myself to hit the pavement to find a new job, $300 poorer from the fines I got slapped with.

Restaurants take the underage drinking problem very seriously, and managers have been known to spot-check a restaurant and card the drinkers. Be wary!

WHAT IF YOU DO GET FIRED?

IT IS ALWAYS SCARY when an authority figure expresses disapproval about your behavior. Being fired might make you feel like you're five years old and you've been sent to the principal's office. But you're in a much better position than that quivering, wet-drawered kindergartner—you have other options! You can get another job! And that is exactly what you should do, since sitting and moaning about how unfair your former bosses are won't do your bank account much good.

But, once you have some distance, try to figure out why you got fired. Is it for the reasons they gave when they booted you out, or is something else going on? Were they justified in firing you? (Of course not! . . . Well, maybe a little?) Is there anything you can do the next time so that it won't happen again? Being able to identify your mistakes and your employer's point of view will help you become a stronger waiter (and a better person). So, if you get fired, take a deep breath, get another job ASAP, then step back and see if you can learn any lessons from the last experience.

DISCRIMINATION

THIS IS AN UNFAIR WORLD, and often the minority can be taken advantage of or misused because of who they are. This section will clue you into some of the things you should be wary of if you're a woman, a person of color, or homosexual.

SEXUAL HARASSMENT AND DISCRIMINATION

Women can face serious sexual harassment in this business, from customers, coworkers, managers, and owners. Because waitresses are servers, some lecherous men can get it into their heads that women should be serving more than food. This is where lack of job security in this industry may actually work in your favor—if you are being harassed in your workplace, you can search for a job elsewhere and then quit more easily than you can in other professions. But being the victim of sexual harassment is always traumatic and infuriating, regardless of whether you can quit the job easily or not.

One waitress was told by her *manager*, as a male coworker looked on in appreciation, that she had "the perfect mouth for oral sex." It's repulsive, it's demeaning, and it happens. One way to deal with it is to nip any inappropriate behavior in the bud. Some women believe that if they ignore it, it will go away. IT WILL NOT GO AWAY. Your manager's lascivious comments about your body will NOT stop if you pretend they don't exist. You HAVE to say something. Don't worry about losing your job, or that the manager won't like you if you say something. Guys who make nasty comments to women are like little boys—they'll actually often respect you more if you seem to have a strong sense of your own self-worth and what you'll accept and what you will not.

Because of this "men are really little boys" phenomenon, you have the moral high ground and can send even the mightiest of managers scampering with his tail between his legs, if you take the right tone. So if someone makes a comment to you, pretend that you're that person's mother or older sister. Say, in a firm voice, and making eye contact, "I don't find that very funny. Do you?" Don't smile. One waitress, when confronted with this situation, whirls around, points a finger at the offender, and says loudly, "Respect!" If silence ensues after you confront him, don't feel compelled to fill it with a quick apology or something. You don't have to take that crap.

Now, you may feel that you're overreacting to an innocent comment made in fun. And you may be right—you can check with the other, older waitresses later to see if the person you had your sexual riff with is a lech or just an inept guy who doesn't know how to make a joke. But note two things: First, overreacting is better than keeping quiet because even if you seem like you "can't take a joke," at least that person will know that he can't make sexist comments around you. Second, if you keep quiet, the offender will never know that he has offended you. He might do it again, making you feel more and more uncomfortable each time.

Discrimination also exists. One waitress had to put up with bad stations and fewer shifts per week than her male coworkers because, as her manager patiently explained to her, "Women just aren't as competent as men."

Your level of comfort is the important thing. As a general rule, any comment, or gesture, or action that makes you feel uncomfortable is probably out of line. Different people have different comfort levels—one woman's insult is another woman's hilarious joke. It all depends on you and how you feel. But, to hammer in this point, if you ever feel uncomfortable with something, and you feel like you're being harassed, you *must* say something, to prevent yourself from being uncomfortable every time you're around that person. Prepare your response *now*, before it happens.

> **Q:** Why should you be forced to leave a perfectly good job because some caveman is making inappropriate comments to you?
>
> **A:** You shouldn't.

RACIAL DISCRIMINATION

Even though some white Americans would like to see most people of color having jobs exclusively in the service industry, discrimination in restaurant hiring practices and staff treatment still occurs. Read the section above on how women should deal with harassing comments, and apply the same technique for anyone who makes any even remotely racist remarks. You might get a reputation for being "touchy," but so what? But make sure that you're a competent server, and an honest one at that. Because when something goes wrong at the restaurant, it's easy for them to blame the person who looks different. If it gets really bad, look for a job somewhere else. And consider whether you have the stomach and the time for a lawsuit.

DISCRIMINATION AGAINST HOMOSEXUALS

Your lifestyle is your own business, and if it has no effect on your quality of service, it is not a topic for discussion unless you want it to be. Gay waiters I interviewed agreed that for some reason, people sometimes feel it's okay to ask very personal questions out of the blue. It is *not* okay if it makes you feel uncomfortable. You can and should draw the line. You can say, "I would prefer not to discuss that," and stay quiet. If that doesn't work, and you're not sure how else to go about asserting your rights, look at the section above telling women how to deal with harassment. But if anyone give you trouble about your sexual orientation, tell them where to go. Right is on your side.

PUBLIC AND PRIVATE: WORK AND YOUR PERSONAL LIFE

EVERYONE'S LIFE IS FULL OF DRAMA, and everyone has bad days. Make every effort not to let these days weave their way into your work. If your boyfriend dumps you and you can't function, find people to cover your shifts or take a little time off. Don't start crying at work or give your tables away during your shift because you're "just not up to it." Even if your manager knows you're going through a rough time, chances are she won't be very understanding if you stop pulling your weight. Work is work. Think about it: If you stop functioning at work because of personal problems, your manager will start doubting your ability to handle other tough situations that arise at the restaurant (drunk customers, a fire). When times are rough, do your best to keep your personal problems personal. Do not let them affect your work.

WHAT IF YOU HATE IT?

And you might hate it. The MegaBucks Waiter quiz should have given you some idea of what it would be like to serve people and work with sit-com characters. But before you quit, remember that with any job there is an adjustment period to go through. It usually takes *at least* a month to be comfortable in your new environment. Then, if you still can't stand your job, try to identify why you hate it. Is it because you can't stand being at the customer's beck and call? Is it because you are very bad at remembering to do many things at the same time? Is it because you can't stop dropping hot liquids on customers, and will soon be fired? Whatever the reason, figure it out, then talk to either a manager or one of the veteran waiters at the restaurant to see how the problem can be resolved. An experienced observer can offer a perspective you don't have. You may just need a little practice. Maybe this restaurant has the wrong vibe for your aura. And yes, maybe you should quit the profession altogether. But don't try to ride it out without talking to someone and making yourself feel better. You may find that your problem is common among new waiters. But, if you don't talk to anyone, you will be miserable.

And nobody tips miserable people, so you won't even be making money. As you'll soon find out, a good mood on the job magically improves your level of service, and you will often see the difference in the tips you make! So don't stick with the job if, after you explore all the reasons, you still hate it. There are lots of other jobs to choose from, and you can find one that doesn't eat away at your soul.

THE LIFESTYLE

THE TYPICAL PERSON WAITING TABLES is under thirty, single, and kind of transient. Since most people go out to eat in restaurants at night, most waiters work at night. As a result, the atmosphere of the industry is very "party" oriented. It is easy for waiters to fall into a lifestyle of sleeping by day, working at night, and partying into the wee hours of the morning. This is a lot of fun, and you can meet a lot of people, but you should be wary. There is a lot of alcohol and drug abuse in the industry, which is magnified by the fact that you are constantly serving people out to have a good time.

People who wait tables for a living tend to live off the dollars they walk home with, paying their rent with cash, and using money orders to cover their credit card bills. Saving money is tough in a cash-and-carry lifestyle. You may turn around six months after you begin waiting tables and realize that even though you have been Mr. MegaBucks in tips every night, you have no savings.

WHAT IF YOU GET STUCK WAITING TABLES FOREVER?

This job can suck you in. Good money with no advanced degrees or rigid hours is a seductive lure. Many waiters talk about the dangers of waiting tables for too long. You are making great money, having fun, and the next thing you know, it's two years later. Your motivation to enter the career you really wanted has vanished during your two-year spree. Changing career paths would mean a significant dip in income. You wonder how you got there.

Don't get sucked in like this—it's really hard to get out! If you're hurting for money but want to start on your other career track, you could pick up a couple of cocktail shifts at night to make some extra pocket change. You'll be tired, but the money that you crave will be there.

Part V

Conclusion

WELL, THAT'S IT—everything you need to know to get up and running (and you will be running) as a waiter. You'll find that some of the advice in this book may not work for you personally as you get into your own pace at your restaurant, and you'll start to develop your *own* short-cuts and operating instructions as you become a better waiter. In fact, there will come a time when you feel like you've really gotten the hang of this job—where you have a full station, you've even picked up tables for someone else who's not feeling well, and you know what's going on with *every* customer: you are ON TOP OF IT. That feeling of mastery is a great thing in any job, but it's particularly satisfying here, since your smug sense of well-being will probably translate into good tips for the night.

Hopefully this book has helped make your first job as a waiter easier and more understandable so that making the good money comes more quickly for you. This book is all about anticipating what people will want from you— so good for you for reading this book to get background on the industry you're entering! Not everyone does that kind of research, so you should be proud of yourself for getting a jump on the competition.

Waiting tables requires a lot of patience, volition, and very thick skin. Abuse comes from random people—and, of course, you are supposed to grin and bear it. But this job is fun. You have a unique opportunity to interact with many different kinds of people and learn new things while making great money. A friend of mine said that waiting tables is about not panicking when everything is going wrong. She learned that she can handle anything, and so can you. All you have to do is remember to be alert to your customers' needs and manage the demands on your time. You'll remember your experiences in a restaurant for the rest of your life.

To order more copies of *"Waiter, There's a Fly in My Soup"*, see the last page. If you want to get in touch with me to comment on the book or on life or anything, please write to:

Leslie N. Lewis
PO Box 20155
West Village Station
New York, NY 10014
Or e-mail me at LeslieLew@aol.com.
I'd love to hear from you.

Enjoy and good luck!

EXTRAS

ALCOHOLIC BEVERAGES

COMMON DRINKS
The Liquors They Contain and Typical Garnishes

Bloody Mary: Vodka with tomato juice spiced with Tabasco and various other goodies. Garnished with a wedge of lemon/lime and a celery stick.

Cape Codder: Vodka and cranberry juice. Garnish with a slice of lime.

Daiquiri: Rum, lime juice✤, garnished with a wedge of lime. Also frozen or on the rocks, and can be made with strawberries, bananas, pineapple, and a variety of other fruits and garnished with any of those fruits.

Kamikaze: Vodka, Triple Sec, lime juice, garnished with a lime.

Manhattan: Whiskey and sweet vermouth with a cherry

Margarita: Tequila and Triple Sec with lime juice, sour mix and a lime wedge. Can be frozen, on the rocks, or straight up.

✤ "Lime juice" in a bar isn't what you get when you squeeze those little green citrus fruits—it's a bottle of lime-flavored syrup. Funny, huh?

Martini: Vodka or gin with a drop of dry vermouth, garnished with an olive. A Gibson is a martini garnished with a cocktail onion.

Melon Ball: Vodka, Midori, and OJ, garnished with lemon

Mimosa: Champagne, OJ, garnished with a strawberry/orange, etc.

Rob Roy: Scotch and dry vermouth garnished with lemon.

Screwdriver: Vodka and OJ. No garnish.

Seabreeze: Vodka, cranberry, and grapefruit, garnished with a lime.

Sex on the Beach: Peach schnapps, vodka, OJ, and cranberry garnished with a condom. Just kidding. There's generally no condom when you have sex on the beach.

Tom Collins: Gin, sour mix and soda.

White Russian: Vodka, kahlua and milk. No garnish.

POPULAR BRANDS
Call Brands of Common Liquors

Bourbons: Jack Daniels, Wild Turkey.

Gins: Tanqueray, Beefeater, Bombay Gin, Bombay Sapphire.

Rums: Bacardi, Malibu, Captain Morgan, Meyers Dark.

Tequilas: Cuervo, Sauza, Patron Anejo Gold.

Vodkas: Absolut, Smirnoff, Stolichnaya (also known as Stoli), Finlandia.

Whiskeys (Scotch): Johnny Walker Red Label, Johnny Walker Black Label, Glenfiddich, Chivas Regal, Dewars, J & B.

Whiskeys (Canadian): Crown Royal, Canadian Club, Seagrams.

Whiskeys (Irish): Jamesons, Black Bush.

EXTRAS B
A GUIDING LIGHT TO WINE

KNOWING YOUR WINES can make your job more lucrative. Your suggestion of a harmonious wine to your customers not only increases the dollar amount of the check, but also gives them a great taste to go along with their meal.

If you're working in an upscale restaurant, there may be a wine waiter or sommelier who takes care of wine orders. On the other hand, if you're working in a very informal place, there may only be house red and house white by the glass or carafe and a few wines offered by the bottle. Most likely you'll end up working at a restaurant somewhere in between.

You should learn about the wines your restaurant stocks so you can discuss them intelligently with your customers. Some restaurants provide training for this. Bartenders are usually more than happy to brag about their wine knowledge, so feel free to ask. If you learn your wines, you'll not only be a more valuable waiter, but you can also impress your dates!

Everyone knows the formula: Red wine with red meats and white wine with fish and poultry. That's a very basic rule, and some of your customers may well choose to break it.

There's no crash course in wines, but here are some fundamental distinctions between wines that will help you on the job.

Since wines begin with a grape, that's where we'll start. When the wine is named after the grape, it's called a *varietal*. When it's named after the place where it was grown, it's called a *regional* wine. Most French wines are regional—for instance Bordeaux is a region of France—ditto Burgundy. In the rest of the world, wines are mostly varietals and are more usually named for the grape rather than the region. Some popular grapes used to make wine are:

RED WINE GRAPES	WHITE WINE GRAPES

Cabernet Sauvignon
(cah-ber-NAY soh-vee-NYON)

The most popular and well-known red wine grape. Makes regional Bordeaux wines in France, often in combination with other grapes. Makes varietal wines in California, Australia, Chile, Argentina, usually called, you guessed it, cabernet sauvignon, or just Cabernet.

Merlot (mur-LOH)

Wine made from this grape has had a recent boom in popularity. The wine tends to be less harsh, more soft and approachable than Caber-net. In France, merlot is found in Bordeaux. In California, merlot-made wines are sometimes called "Meritage", probably because it sounds French.

Pinot Noir (PEE-noh NWAHR)

This grape makes red burgundy wines, which are very good with many kinds of food. It is not as dark as cabernet.

Zinfandel
(ZIN-fan-del, silly!)

These grapes make a very dark wine that tends to be fruity. Good with spicy foods. Do not confuse them with white zinfandel, the sweet, slightly fizzy, pink wine invented in 1972 by a Californian.

Sauvignon Blanc
(SOH-vee-NYON BLON)

This grape tends to make crisp, refreshing, aromatic wines which are very good as an aperitif. In the U.S., this grape makes wines called sauvignon blanc or fumé blanc (pronounced FOO-may BLON). In the rest of the world, the wine is just called sauvignon blanc or it's named after its region, if it's French.

Riesling
(REEZE-ling)

If it's an Alsatian Riesling, it is probably dry and very good with food— especially spicy food. If it is a German Riesling, it is probably sweeter, and good for dessert or an aperitif. If it's from the U.S., it might be called Johannisberg, Rhine, or white Riesling, and it's probably sweeter, and therefore good for dessert or aperitif. Rieslings have gained in popularity recently, too.

Chardonnay
(SHAR-doh-nay)

Almost synonymous with white wine in the United States, this is a popular generally fruity wine if American, but more subtle if French. The chardonnay grape makes white burgundies in France, chardonnay everywhere else.

THE CHARACTERISTICS AND TYPES OF DIFFERENT WINES

There are so many varieties of wine that it is hard to generalize about their quality, but here are a few standard benchmarks.

Following Your Nose

Wines have all sorts of flavors and qualities that can be used to describe them. Thus there are many terms for how a wine smells (its nose or bouquet) and how it tastes (fruity, full bodied, and so on.) What's important for you is to know your restaurant's wine list and be able to make informed suggestions when asked. The food list coming up will help you with that

People who know their wine will just go ahead and order what they want. If they do have a question about a particular wine that you can't knowledgeably answer, bluff, or ask someone who knows.

As for people who don't know wines, try and find out what their price range is. Then you can match them up with the perfect wine for their meal.

Whites

Dry (not sweet) or medium-dry white wines are preferred for the main meal. The common ones are sauvignon blanc, Chablis, chardonnay, and Riesling. These may come from all over the world. Most white wines are served chilled and are kept at the table in a bucket of ice.

Sweet white wines such as sauterne are usually drunk with dessert. Dessert wines are not served chilled. Champagne, usually reserved for dessert, can sometimes served be throughout the meal. Real Champagne only comes from the Champagne region of France and is never sweet. Anything else is sparkling wine, regardless of how expensive the bottle looks, and it may be sweet or dry. Suggest bubbly to a table for a birthday celebration or any special occasion.

Reds

Red wines are usually fairly dry. They are properly served at room temperature. Your customer might ask you to let a red wine "breathe," or sit open, for a while before they start drinking it. It often tastes better this way—suggest it to your other customers.

Purists often stick with French wines, and when suggesting one to a customer, you can't go wrong. Red wines spring from many different parts of France. On an American wine list the main sources are the Bordeaux, Burgundy, and Côtes du Rhône regions. Bordeaux wines, known as clarets, have an enormous range of characteristics, from light- to full-bodied.

Burgundy wines are usually more full-bodied and can be a good choice to serve with red meats and strong sauces. Beaujolais wines from the Burgundy region are excellent with light lunches. Late each fall, you may hear a lot about the fashionable *Beaujolais nouveau*—new Beaujolais from that year flown in from France. Being a very young wine, it is served slightly chilled. Côtes du Rhône wines are quite popular and include the famous Châteauneuf du Pape.

Other reds: While Chianti is the best known Italian wine, Italy does produce a great variety of reds (and whites). Spain produces good wine, the best known of which is Rioja.

California produces lots of reds. Some are very good and others are jug wine (a.k.a. cheap booze). Good California wines mostly use varieties of French and Italian grapes and try to match or better their

European cousins—they tend to be expensive. Chilean and Argentinian, as well as Australian and South African, reds have also become popular because usually they're a good buy.

Red dessert wines include port and Madiera.

Rosé or Blush Wines

Rosé or blush wines are often considered the "trailer trash" of the vintage community, a bastard wine-lite that makes true aficionados wince. But rosés (like wine coolers) can be pleasant for light summer meals because they are served cold, and because they are pink.

Other Wines

Other curious wines include vino verde (literally green wine), a light white from Portugal that is good with fish and seafood. Retsina, a white wine from Greece, is flavored with a resin that gives it a slightly woody taste.

WINE TERMS

Bouquet: The smell of the wine. Something with a heady bouquet, for example, is a full-bodied wine; wine with a more fruity or light bouquet is milder.

Corked: When the seal between the cork and the bottle has been breached and the wine has spoiled in some way.

Dry: The opposite of sweet; there are varying degrees of dryness.

Legs: When the wine is swirled around the glass, its "legs" refer to how well the wine hugs the walls of the glass. A wine with good legs is a better wine.

Vintage: The year of production; some years the wine is better than others.

FOOD COMBINATIONS

Remember—these are just suggestions. Your customers can drink whatever they want, of course.

Aperitifs:

Champagne, sherry, dry white wine, Madeira, vermouths. Aperitifs are drinks before the meal, used to whet the appetite, sharpen the palate, and get those stomach juices flowing.

Appetizers/FingerFoods/Hors d'Oeuvres:

Suggest sauvignon blanc or sherry—why not?

Pasta and Rice Dishes:

Chianti or other Italian red wines. Presumably, since the Italians perfected pasta, they know the best wine to go with it.

Fish

Dry white wines, maybe even Champagne. If the fish is cooked in a red wine sauce, then suggest a wine from the same grape type.

White Meats

(Chicken, turkey, veal, pork, bunny rabbit): If the dish is served hot, you can offer a lighter red wine, like a Beaujolais, a New Zealand Pinot Noir, or a California zinfandel, for example. For cold dishes, perhaps suggest a sauvignon blanc—or a fuller white wine.

Red Meats:

Now's the time to bring in the heavy hitting reds, like cabernet sauvignons, Pinot Noirs—especially the big Burgundies from France. Also suggest Côtes du Rhône wines, particularly Châteauneuf du Pape. If the dish is served with a wine-based sauce, you can suggest a wine made with the same grape as the wine in the sauce.

If your customer knows a little bit about wine, but wants your help, go beyond the typical suggestion of chardonnay for white, cabernet for a red. Try offering Riesling for white, Pinot Noir for red. These wines are known to be extremely food friendly, and your customer will feel cutting-edge trying a wine that's uncommon for the average drinker.

SOME WINE TIPS

These are just guidelines, not hard-and-fast rules. But deploy them with your customer and you'll sound like a stud.

White wines before red. Dry wines before sweet.

Young wines before old.

Pants before shoes. Zinfandels for spicy food.

WINE ETIQUETTE

The following is the standard procedure for opening and serving wine.

When you approach the table, show the label on the wine bottle to the person who chose the wine. This is done to confirm that you are serving the customer the correct bottle. Wine should always be uncorked at the table, and never turn your back on the customer. Wrap a linen napkin around the neck of the bottle. Use the knife on your waiter's corkscrew (called a wine key) to carve off the top of the foil covering the cork and the neck of the bottle. Once the cork is exposed, you twist the corkscrew into the bottle with one hand, holding the bottle firmly with the other (it's best to go in from an angle, then straighten the wine key once the tip of the screw is in—then you can start turning in earnest). Ease the cork out slowly, bracing yourself for the final little "pop," so that no wine will spill on you or the customer.

If they have ordered a bottle of Champagne, the rules for opening the bottle change a bit. First, you have to remove the wire cork restrainer. This is usually easy to do. Look under the foil covering the bottle neck for the ring that untwists the wire hood. Once the wire is off, cover the cork and neck of the bottle with your napkin, and put your fist around the cork. Grasp the bottle with one hand and ease the cork out *gently* with the other hand. Use a slow twisting and rocking motion. The cork should be restrained by your hand and the napkin as it pushes itself out with a slow pop. Make sure the Champagne is well chilled when you do this, or you will have a little fountain—maybe even a broken window—from the pressure of the warm gasses against the escaping cork. Remember, this is not practice for New Year's Eve. Never aim a bottle at your customers, no matter how annoying they are. The aim is to hear a soft "pop"—not blind a customer with the cork while half of the Champagne gushes onto the floor.

After a bottle is open, pour a small amount of the wine or Champagne into the glass of the person who chose it. Then remove the cork from the corkscrew, and present it with aplomb to the taster. She should taste the wine and tell you if it is acceptable to serve. If the wine taster accepts the wine, pour everyone else's glass one-third to half full. Start with the women at the table, then serve the men, and finish with the taster. After filling a glass, flick your wrist gently, turning the neck of the bottle as you tilt the bottle up to finish pouring—this prevents spillage. Then, if it's a bottle of white, Champagne, or rosé, you thrust the bottle into the ice bucket you brought with you, and leave the napkin draped across the top of the bucket. If it's a bottle of red, which does not get chilled, you leave the bottle on the table, with the napkin beside it.

If the taster says the wine is corked or complains that it is unsatisfactory in some other way, apologize and get your manager. Leave the bottle where it is and let someone more experienced deal with that problem.

Keep an eye out to see that your customers' glasses are refilled—but never too full. (Don't pour the last drops of wine from a bottle of red, as it may have a sediment that tastes gross.) If the table orders a second bottle of wine, you should bring out a new round of glasses, and the taster should taste again. It is up to that person whether you should use the new glasses, or whether the wine is similar enough to be poured into the same glasses as before.

Some customers, when they really enjoy a wine, like to bring the label home with them. If you have to remove the label, just let the bottle soak in a bucket of water for a minute and the label should peel right off.

If you don't feel comfortable selling wines to your customers, ask another waiter to take over your table or give you a hand. But after a few occasions opening a wine bottle and suggesting wines to a customer, your comfort level, as well as the average price of your checks, will increase rapidly. You'll get the hang of it.

AFTER-DINNER DRINKS

Offer these to your customers after dessert or when you take their coffee orders. Other than dessert wines like sauturne and port, there are two kinds of after-dinner drinks that also will add considerably to your customers' tab:

Spirits: The popular ones are cognac, Armagnac, brandy, and grappa. It's a particularly good idea to know what cognacs the bar stocks, as some customers will order these by name (Remy Martin, Courvoisier, Delamain, etc.). If they don't, you can make a suggestion—remember some are very expensive, so don't oversell.

Liqueurs: There are hundreds of these sweet, often brightly colored, drinks that have a brandy or other spirit base mixed with sugar and natural flavorings. You'll soon learn the names of the popular ones such as Cointreau, Kalua, Benedictine, and Bailey's Irish Cream. Some of them can be served with ice, but let your customer make that request.

GLOSSARY

Call liquor: Alcohol with a brand name people recognize, like Absolut or Dewars. A call liquor is the opposite of a bar (or "well") liquor—which is the cheapest kind of antifreeze the restaurant can buy without violating FDA regulations.

Cash and carry: Paying scheme where you do not run tabs when supplying customers with drinks. You, instead, cash out each check as it's ordered. Used for cocktailing.

Deuce: A table that seats two people.

Eight-Six: Out of stock.

Fine dining: Generally refers to restaurants of a certain level of class. Some identifying traits are high prices, snazzy uniforms for the staff, silverware and glasses already on the table, and a general level of snootiness. If the place has tablecloths and the busboys fill water glasses, it's probably fine dining.

Four-top: Table for four.

In the weeds: When you're so busy you can barely function properly. Example: "I'm so in the weeds." Generally not followed by any further description because you're too busy to chit-chat.

On the fly: Used mostly by cooks and expediters. Means "right away" when talking about the speed needed for preparation of a certain table's food.

Running: When your customers' demands have kept you on the move all day, with no time for a break.

Slammed: When all of a sudden your entire section is full and you're weeded.

Turn-and-Burn: Any restaurant where waiters will harass customers if they stay longer than an hour and a half, if they're not buying huge quantities of food.

Weeded: Can be used interchangeably with "In the weeds."

EXTRAS D
COMMON FOOD PREPARATION TERMS

If you're not used to going out to restaurants to eat, or if Julia Child isn't a close friend, you may not know some words often used to describe food preparation. These words are helpful for the Arbiter of Taste aspect of your job—you can make oatmeal sound exotic simply by changing your vocabulary.

Baste: To moisten a food with gravy or some other sauce while it's cooking.

Blanch: To boil a food rapidly and very briefly, in order to preserve color, remove bacteria, seal in juices, or help remove shells or peels.

Caramelize: To heat sugars until they turn caramel-colored and gain a different flavor.

Clarify: To separate and remove solids from a liquid, like butter. This is done so that the resulting liquid is harder to burn.

Fricassee: To stew foods gently in liquids and vegetables.

Poach: To simmer gently in water. Poached eggs, for example, or poached salmon.

Sear: To quickly thrust meat into high heat so that its juices are sealed in.

EXTRAS E
HOW TO HOLD YOUR LIQUOR
(on a tray, silly!)

If your restaurant requires you to bring out all the food on trays, they may teach you themselves how to do it properly. But, if you don't get any formal training, there are some things you should know.

There are three main ways to hold a tray. Two are acceptable, and one makes intuitive sense but is just plain wrong. Let's start with that one, hmm?

Do not pick up a tray with two hands and put it down on your customer's table when you take food or drinks to their table (Fig. 1). This is a very big no-no. It looks bad, it's seen as sloppy, and it will not please your managers. You should always carry a tray with one hand only, so that if you need to take something off the tray, and you don't have anywhere to set it down, you can use your other hand. Here are the two right ways to carry a tray single-handedly: First, if you're not carrying too much stuff, you can balance the tray on your fingertips. This allows you to keep the tray steady, since your five fingers can correct for any imbalance, like a tripod—or a pentapod, as the case may be (Fig 2).

The second way to carry a tray is a little more tricky and might require practice at home, where you won't be dropping stuff on customers. You balance the tray on your flat palm, then twist your wrist up and around so that your fingers are now pointing backwards and the tray is parallel with your shoulder. If the tray is really heavy, you can balance it on your shoulder for extra support (Fig. 3). There is more support in this way of holding your tray: Get comfortable with it.

The tricky part about carrying a tray this way is the twisting of the wrist to get it up to your shoulder and back down again. Practice . . . practice . . . practice.

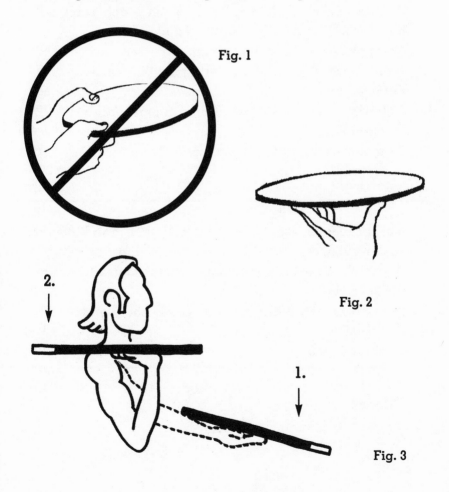

Fig. 1

Fig. 2

2.

1.

Fig. 3

WHERE TO WORK

Here are some of the more popular summer and winter resort areas in the United States that flood with tourists and the waitstaff who serve them.

Winter

Florida, especially Miami Beach, Palm Beach, Daytona Beach, the Florida Keys, and Ft. Lauderdale
Colorado, especially Aspen and Vail
Utah, especially Park City during the Sundance Film Festival
California, especially Lake Tahoe, Squaw Valley, and Sun Valley
Vermont, especially Killington and Okemo

Summer

Massachusetts, especially Nantucket, Martha's Vineyard, Boston's Faneuil Hall, Harvard Square, and Cape Cod
New York, especially the Hamptons, the Catskills, and the Poconos
New Jersey, especially the New Jersey shore and Atlantic City
Virginia Beach

INDEX

THE AUTHOR

Ever since she was little, Leslie N. Lewis has been fascinated by the restaurant business. Her father regaled her with stories of his adventures waiting tables as a teenager in the country club where his grandfather was head waiter. Mr. Lewis later went on to own TLC Beatrice International, a multi-national food conglomerate where Ms. Lewis has been a director since 1991.

While attending Harvard College, Ms. Lewis worked on two academic case studies of local restaurants for school credit. She was also a reporter for the weekly news magazine, *The Independent*, and a researcher-writer assigned the arduous beat of the French Riviera for the top-selling travel guide, *Let's Go Europe*.

After graduating in 1995, she drove to Miami and waited tables at South Beach's popular grill, the News Café. There she gained the experience that inspired this book.

Ms. Lewis also writes fiction, including screenplays and several short stories. She is currently working on her first novel, and will be attending film school in the fall of 1997.

CONTRIBUTORS

EDITOR

Lauren Monaco works at Simon & Schuster in New York City. While in high school and college, she was also a waitress for seven years—and yes, after college too.

ARTISTS

Ly Bolia is a New York City-based storyboard artist and cinematographer.

Keith Knight is a San Francisco Bay area–based cartoonist whose comic strip, **The K Kronicles**, is distributed nationally. For a catalogue of Keith Knight's cartoons, send a S.A.S.E. to P.O. Box 591794, San Francisco, CA 94159-1794.

Leslie Jowett is an artist working in New York City.

Thomas Shelford is an illustrator based in New York City. He can be reached at (212) 941-6869.

TO ORDER MORE COPIES of
this book, call customer service
BOOKMARK PUBLISHING at
(800) 247-6553. They're open twenty
four hours a day, seven days a week and they accept
American Express, MasterCard, Visa, and Discover cards.

"Waiter, There's a Fly in My Soup"
is set in Memphis Medium and Light.
Memphis, which dates from 1929, was part of
the popular Egyptian, or slab serif, revival
that resulted in a classicism peculiar to the U.S.
The face was designed by Dr. Rudolph Wolf
for the Stempel foundry.

Photo: Angela Cappetta

LESLIE N. LEWIS, born in 1973,
is a director of TLC Beatrice
International Foods.

THE *ULTIMATE* REFERENCE GUIDE TO WAITING TABLES

✤ **For anybody who wants to break into the restaurant industry.**

✤ **For students and graduates who need to earn extra cash.**

✤ **For all waiters (novice to experienced) who want to perfect their skills.**

✤ **For every diner: Find out what your waiter's *really* thinking.**

This handbook has great advice. If you read this and your name is Charlie Smith or Ralph Wollensky, I would hire you in a New York minute!
—Alan N. Stillman, Chief Cook & Bottle Washer
SMITH & WOLLENSKY, NYC

"Waiter, There's a Fly in My Soup" is a must-read for anyone who wants to wait tables—and have fun trying. This book shows us that you can laugh and learn how to get into the restaurant business all at the same time.
—Patrick Clark, Executive Chef
TAVERN ON THE GREEN, NYC

I wish I'd had this book when I started waiting, but at least I have it now. Lewis' common sense approach to waiting tables will benefit all who read the book.
—Kenneth Cornick
TRIBECA GRILL

$ 8.95 U.S.
$12.95 Canada

BOOKMARK PUBLISHING CORP.
P.O. BOX 2100 AMANGANSETT, NY 11930
(800) 247-6553

Cover design: Tenth Avenue Editions
Cover Illustration: Keith Knight